mcLuhan
for managers

mcLuhan for managers

NEW THINKING

NEW TOOLS FOR

mark federman
derrick de kerckhove

Viking
CANADA

VIKING CANADA

Penguin Group (Canada), a division of Pearson Penguin Canada Inc., 10 Alcorn Avenue, Toronto, Ontario M4V 3B2

Penguin Group (U.K.), 80 Strand, London WC2R 0RL, England
Penguin Group (U.S.), 375 Hudson Street, New York, New York 10014, U.S.A.
Penguin Group (Australia) Inc., 250 Camberwell Road, Camberwell, Victoria 3124, Australia
Penguin Group (Ireland), 25 St. Stephen's Green, Dublin 2, Ireland
Penguin Books India (P) Ltd, 11, Community Centre, Panchsheel Park, New Delhi – 110 017, India
Penguin Group (New Zealand), cnr Rosedale and Airborne Roads, Albany, Auckland 1310, New Zealand
Penguin Books (South Africa) (Pty) Ltd, 24 Sturdee Avenue, Rosebank 2196, South Africa

Penguin Group, Registered Offices: 80 Strand, London WC2R 0RL, England

First published 2003

1 2 3 4 5 6 7 8 9 10 (FR)

Manufactured in Canada.

National Library of Canada Cataloguing in Publication

Federman, Mark
    McLuhan for managers : new tools for new thinking / Mark Federman, Derrick de Kerckhove.

Includes bibliographical references and index.

ISBN 0-670-04371-0

    1. Management. 2. Creative thinking. 3. Creative ability in business.
I. De Kerckhove, Derrick II. Title.

HD31.F43 2003   658.4   C2003-902798-8

Visit the Penguin Group (Canada) website at **www.penguin.ca**

To our children, David and Julie,
and Charles and Dak

Contents

Acknowledgments

During the journey that resulted in the creation of this work, many people have shared guidance and insight. To each of them we owe a debt of gratitude. Eric McLuhan planted the initial seed of inspiration by focusing us on the Laws of Media and raising the possibility that they could be directly applied to business concerns and problems. We greatly appreciate his ongoing support, suggestions and encouragement of this project.

Several people donated considerable time and thought in reviewing our early draft of the manuscript. To Adriana Ieraci, Misha Sivan and John Male we offer our sincere thanks for your excellent efforts and advice. Two reviewers went far above and beyond the call of duty in their assistance. Arnold Wytenburg challenged our thinking at every turn and offered invaluable suggestions and guidance. As a result, we were able to uncover some of the most interesting discoveries throughout the book. Christine Sorenson spent many hours in correspondence and discussion, helping us work through many concepts and assisting with test cases for many of our examples. The book is considerably richer thanks to her contributions. Thanks also to Andrew McCutcheon and Agnes Kruchio who listened patiently to our frequent rants that prompted many of our avenues of investigation.

Over the gestational period, dozens of people were (sometimes unwitting) guinea pigs as we refined the thinking tools in various playshops. To these unsung heroes, we say, "Thanks for playing."

The staff at Viking Canada have been wonderful to work with and tremendously supportive of our project. Sincere appreciation to Ed Carson, Andrea Crozier, Susan Folkins, Joe Zingrone, and Catherine Dorton. Thanks to our editor, Nancy Carroll, for her precision and attention to detail in the manuscript. Thanks also to Robert Mackwood for his excellent efforts on our behalf.

We offer our sincere appreciation and gratitude to the Estate of Marshall McLuhan, Corinne McLuhan, and Mo Cohen of Gingko Press for their support of our work and kind permission to quote from the many aphorisms and works of Marshall McLuhan.

Finally, we thank our wives, Miriam and Marnie, and our families for their indulgence, understanding and support during the many long hours of research, writing, editing, rewriting and absence in our "garret."

Foreword

One of the delightful anomalies of our future-obsessed digital age is the quiet resurgence of 1960s icon Marshall McLuhan as the prophet of the transformations afoot today. Silicon Valley twenty-somethings who were infants when McLuhan passed away in 1980 invoke his name in meetings and insert his aphorisms in their business plans. Indeed, the ghost of McLuhan haunts the entire Internet revolution.

This interest in McLuhan is understandable, for McLuhan's ideas were astoundingly prescient. The 1960s' Sage of Aquarius not only defined the mass media age of TV, he also anticipated much of the personal media revolution to follow. Decades before the first PC arrived, he foretold a coming age of home computers and electronic alternatives to grocery shopping. And long before the term "new economy" entered our vocabulary, he pointed to the inevitable acceleration of economic life that would accompany the new electronic media, detailing not only the changing nature of money, but also the risks to governments and societies from business conducted at "electric speed." If only we had read McLuhan more carefully, perhaps we would have anticipated the opportunity of a George Soros, the brewing disaster of Asian currency meltdown or the up (and down) of the dot–com bubble.

And there lies the rub. McLuhan is not just dazzlingly prescient, but also dizzyingly vague and maddeningly impenetrable. It is easier to discover what McLuhan meant after events have unfolded than to unwrap outcomes from his double entendres and gnomic pronouncements. The consequence is that McLuhan is more often quoted than read; and even when read, he is rarely understood in a way that leads to useful action. Worse yet, McLuhan is not merely misunderstood, but his ideas are too often put to the service of something he particularly detested — a nostalgic "living in the rear-view mirror." Dwelling on McLuhan's track record as prognosticator is thus not merely pointless; it is an invitation to be blindsided by the future.

The secret to McLuhan is this: His genius lay more in how he thought than in what he anticipated. Hidden in his vast body of work is a way of looking at our shape-shifting world to reveal the myriad transformations lurking around the corner. McLuhan is not an oracle to be consulted, but an intellectual springboard from which to make one's own conceptual leaps of insight and intuition.

The authors of this book blow the lid off McLuhan's secret. They have mined his writings and have done a masterful job of setting out McLuhan's core ideas clearly and in the context of our current digital challenges. But this is just the backdrop to their real task: articulating a set of thinking tools based on McLuhan's unique way of assessing the future.

It is these tools that make this book particularly useful to business decision makers. Business decision makers? Hardly the first audience that comes to mind when thinking about McLuhan, but it turns out that McLuhan's ideas and approach to forecasting are potent business tools for our uncertain times. Business today is about vision — the ability to look ahead and identify the subtle indicators of fundamental changes lurking on the horizon. McLuhan accomplished this with extraordinary skill, applying his unique blend of tools, from noticing the unnoticed, to structured questioning and investigatory "probes."

McLuhan is thus very relevant to business, but there is more to the story of this book than the mere presentation of powerful new business tools. McLuhan was concerned with the impact of technology on culture and society, and of course business is a foundational part of the social equation. In the 1960s, this seemed a radical idea; today it is taken for granted to such a degree that we demand that our business leaders and the companies they guide step up to ever higher standards of social responsibility. Business is no longer just about doing well; it is also about doing good in sustainable ways that make sense for both the doer and society at large.

The tools set forth in this book are powerful vehicles in furthering this larger purpose. The farther one sees, the better decisions one can make, both for companies and the societies they exist within. McLuhan often pleaded that he was a mere observer, but of course that was nonsense. The man who reminded us that we lived in an ever shrinking, ever more interdependent world was not an observer, but an activist. What the authors of this book have done is deliver far-gazing tools for business activists. The electronic revolution's patron saint, the Sage of Aquarius would be pleased.

Paul Saffo
Director and Roy Amara Fellow
Institute for the Future

"Cheshire Puss," [Alice] began. ...
"Would you tell me, please, which
way I ought to go from here?"

"That depends a good deal
on where you want to get to,"
said the Cat.

"I don't much care where —"
said Alice.

"Then it doesn't matter which way
you go," said the Cat.

"— so long as I get somewhere,"
Alice added as an explanation.

"Oh, you're sure to do that," said
the Cat, "if you only walk long
enough."

Lewis Carroll, *Alice's Adventures in Wonderland*

iNtRODUCtiON

I don't explain —
I EXPLORE

— McLuhan Hot and Cool, 1967

Mention the name Marshall McLuhan to most people and they may be able to come up with "The Medium is the Message," "Global Village," and a cameo appearance in Woody Allen's movie, *Annie Hall*. Some may be able to identify him as one of the most important and influential figures among media observers, critics, scientists, theorists and philosophers. It *is* rather difficult to classify McLuhan with any one appellation.

McLuhan was a professor of English Literature. That is about as much as he would admit. He would also acknowledge that he was, from 1963 to 1979, the director of the Centre for Culture and Technology, at the University of Toronto. Every other epithet he was given, such as prophet, philosopher, theorist, media expert, sociologist, even culturologist, he would strenuously oppose. He would become especially irritated when he was dubbed a theorist and snap back: "I have no theory, only observations."[1] An observer, he surely was, but observer is not a profession; it is a condition.

> **McLuhan's unique ability to perceive that which no one else could makes his insights particularly valuable in a business context.**

One of the authors of this book, Derrick de Kerckhove, spent ten years with McLuhan, off and on, at the Centre for Culture and Technology. During that time, never once did he encounter McLuhan abandoning his observational attitude. The object of McLuhan's scrutiny was the effect of technology on culture. From his observations, he would derive new tools for new thinking.

McLuhan consulted for various businesses and major corporations throughout his life. His unique ability to perceive that which no one else could makes his insights particularly valuable in a business context. We experience the effects of his thinking and work every day, through advertising, for example. We experience what McLuhan predicted: the profound effects of having information instantly available at our beck and call, and being able to communicate electronically with anyone, almost anywhere, at any time across a worldwide communications network. When Marshall McLuhan died on New Year's Eve 1980, we had yet to see the vast proliferation of cable TV, and we had just witnessed the birth of the now ubiquitous personal computer and CDs. The World Wide Web, browsers and dot-com companies were all in the future. But it is McLuhan's work, or more precisely his approach and thinking tools, that provides us with the framework to make sense of these new technologies and their impact that we are now seeing in our current, worldwide business environment.

Although McLuhan would disavow labels such as visionary and prophet, over thirty years ago he predicted:

- The rise of roles, replacing jobs

- The decentralizing effects of "electricity-based" communication

- The transformation of hardware into software

- Constant disruptive change, displacing linear progression and any stable sense of status quo

- Elimination of time and geographical disparities due to instantaneous, global communications

- Average people debuting on the world stage with consumers becoming producers

- The "learning organization" and the requirement of "learning a living"

Marshall McLuhan made his observations and spoke of the resulting consequences over thirty years ago. Suppose he could look around our world today and enlighten us with his observations and insights. How might he influence and guide our thinking about business and technologies? Consider this excerpt from his writings and ask yourself whether it resonates with your recent experience:

> With the acceleration of change, management now takes on entirely new functions. While navigating amidst the unknown is becoming the normal role of the executive, the new need is not merely to navigate but to anticipate effects with their causes.[2]

Daunting challenge, to be sure. To meet such a challenge requires unconventional, new thinking. New thinking necessitates new thinking tools. But we cannot conjure up McLuhan from beyond the grave. We can, however, attempt

Our aim is to assist managers to think about complex issues and challenges using McLuhan's thinking tools to increase awareness, perception and insight.

to understand the way he worked and the thinking tools he employed to gain new awareness, perception and insight into the problems and issues of his day. The purpose of this book is to provide such tools and show how to apply them in today's business environment. Our aim is to assist managers to think about complex issues and practical challenges using the same thinking tools as did McLuhan, and consequently to increase awareness, perception and insight. As with any new tools, these take some practice and experience to master. But once even a modicum of expertise is achieved, the tools themselves become almost second nature, their application almost automatic in looking at difficult problems in entirely new ways.

This, of necessity, means giving up some of our old ways, namely our unquestioning faith in what we have taken to be basic business assumptions. McLuhan's thinking tools challenge us to probe and question everything, including the language we use. For example, when first introduced to his most famous aphorism, "the Medium is the Message,"[3] the casual reader will naturally take the common meanings for Medium — a conveyance of information — and Message — the information content. The meaning of McLuhan's paradox is seemingly obvious; the casual reader, however, has gained no additional awareness, insight or perception.

As we will see, McLuhan's particular use of the terms Medium and Message extends our thinking and thereby opens our minds to entirely new possibilities that encourage new perceptions about even everyday objects. Marshall McLuhan probed the effects of new technologies and innovations on culture and society. Probing and investigating allowed him to make his often astounding observations and predictions. To McLuhan, however, the consequences were not astounding at all — the effects were there all the time, as long as we were willing and able to notice them. Unfortunately, most people were unable to discern them until they were observable from the perspective gained by the passage of time — as McLuhan put it, "through the rear-view mirror."

The first chapter of *McLuhan for Managers* describes McLuhan's involvement with business through his lifetime and provides a unique insight into the man himself. If you are anxious to dive right into the thinking tools themselves, feel free to enjoy this chapter at any time during your exploration of the "Wonderland" of McLuhan's thinking.

Chapter 2 introduces McLuhan's language — the basic and essential tools with which he worked. We extend this in Chapter 3 by playing with "management clichés," those overworked, "trite and true" approaches that often prove to be less effective than working managers might hope.

Chapter 4 introduces the Laws of Media Tetrads, perhaps the most powerful awareness-raising tools in the McLuhanesque kit bag. These, together with what may be his most challenging idea — Media Temperature — are made practical and useful in Chapters 5 through 7 through what we like to call "Applied McLuhanistics." We examine business applications ranging from merchandising and online shopping through hiring strategies and management types. We learn lessons from television and apply them to Internet-based business, and consider mergers and the effects of corporate culture.

There are many other ports of call along the way, including designing a company from the *ground* up. We look ahead to the future, and to the often thorny problems raised when ethics intersect with business. Finally, in Chapter 8, we rise to the challenge of a company's staff thinking collaboratively in a framework we call the Connected Intelligence Playshop.

What happens when business leaders suddenly become aware of hidden effects? What new perceptions and insights are available that can help forge new strategies and business directions? How will the business landscape, including all its participants, change when we can shine a bright light on complex problems and begin to see the non-obvious — what, until now, has been hidden from view? When the business paradigm, whose foundation lies on the slab of nearly century-old assumptions, changes its footings, what then becomes possible?

It is time for "New Tools for New Thinking." Dive right in. We think you will find this book an exhilarating, mind-expanding journey. If some of the concepts seem confusing at first, remember that of his own work McLuhan once remarked: "I don't pretend to understand it. After all, my stuff is very difficult."[4]

Any innovation threatens the equilibrium of existing organization. Understanding Media, 1964

7. Cul BUS

"A new medium is never an addition to an old one, nor does it leave the old one in

peace.

ture IS OUR **INESS**

It never ceases to oppress
the older media
until it finds new shapes and positions for them."

—Understanding Media, 1964

The beginning of Marshall McLuhan's relationship with the corporate world was a revealing false start. It may have begun in Winnipeg at the University of Manitoba, where McLuhan befriended the economist, Tom Easterbrook, when they were both freshmen. They found themselves together at a used bookstore. After lengthy rummaging, both came up to the cashier with a book in hand. McLuhan had selected a textbook on economics; Easterbrook had G.K. Chesterton's *What's Wrong with the World?* They looked at each other's choice, looked at each other and, exchanging books, agreed that each had made the other's more appropriate choice. "This is more like your kind of stuff, " said Easterbrook as he gave McLuhan the Chesterton book. Easterbrook became a respected economist, and McLuhan began his journey of conversion to Catholicism inspired by one of England's most influential converts.

McLuhan became incredibly famous. He even made it to the cover of *Newsweek*, which had this to say:

> Industrialists travel from as far away as Japan and India for audiences in his dishevelled, book-lined office at the University of Toronto. American executives pay him fees of up to $1000 to come to their luncheons of stringy roast beef and preach his often impenetrable sermons on communications...Recently, seventeen Canadian executives – including two presidents and five vice-presidents – paid $150 apiece for the privilege of a two-day seminar with McLuhan in Toronto.[1]

McLuhan was treated as a household name on bumper stickers and in popular TV shows such as *Laugh-In*. As late as 1976, he was still enough of a world star to feature in one of Woody Allen's most endearing films, *Annie Hall*, in which he appears as himself upbraiding a typical New York City academic fop pontificating about McLuhan as if he had actually read him. The French even introduced a neologism, *mcluhanisme*, to designate a probably true but generally incomprehensible insight.

Prime Minister Pierre Elliott Trudeau knew McLuhan well:

> When we began to meet he would say, don't worry about contradictions, look at them as probes, don't try to put me into conflict with my own thoughts. I found it a freeing experience. His thoughts were not essentially political, but they were an effort to explain human behaviour under the impact of a new technology, and I think that some of his intuitions were those of a genius.[2]

Mr. McLuhan Goes to Business

Already, several recent tributes and biographies bear witness to this fame,[3] and abundant critical evaluation is building up a respectable scholarship around and about McLuhan. However, only a few writers pay even-handed attention to his relationships with the business world; most would prefer to see McLuhan only as a creature of the media. For Glenn Willmott, "McLuhan had begun to court the business world long before his mediatized celebrity as Pop philosopher — and with no little success."[4] He reminds us that McLuhan, as early as 1955, had created a small PR concern named "Idea Consultants." Philip Marchand reports:

> McLuhan and Hagon's firm offered creative ideas to businesses and was based on McLuhan's cherished notion than an outsider to a business could often come up with solutions to problems that had evaded the 'experts.' One of their slogans, which has an authentic McLuhanesque ring was 'A headache is a million dollar idea trying to get born. Idea Consultants are obstetricians for these ideas.'[5]

Marchand describes a wide variety of ideas that McLuhan and his partner submitted to various companies. These included soap, shampoo and lotions in single-use, disposable foil capsules; panels in buses and subway cars that would flash the names of stops; ready-to-serve sealed airline dinners available for the general public; package tours to pollen-free areas for hay fever sufferers; and remarkably, pre-taped movies — McLuhan called them "television platters" — for replay on home television sets. There was also a proposal for a television program that would feature public participation in problem solving by dramatizing business problems and offering a reward for the best solution.[6]

And, as biographer Terrence Gordon points out,[7] some of their ideas would eventually become significant businesses in their own right:

- Aluminum soft drink containers
- Cartons for alcoholic beverages
- Frozen diet dinners
- Motor-powered pencil sharpeners

A headache is a million dollar idea trying to get born. Idea Consultants slogan, 1955

And, of course, videotapes. But despite their creative and viable ideas, something must have been wrong with their marketing strategies: Idea Consultants didn't sell a single idea and had to close in its second year of operation.

Marketing Marshall McLuhan

All biographers seem to concur that McLuhan owed his world fame to the help of clever ad people and media consultants such as Howard Gossage and Eugene Schwartz. For Donald Theall, however, it is really Tom Wolfe, with his very popular article, "What If He Is Right?,"[8] who fired the initial salvo:

> Wolfe clearly provided a platform for launching McLuhan, Inc. and that platform not only transformed McLuhan into the public media image of a universal guru but created a new place for iconoclastic academics lured by power to join the ranks of media celebrities.[9]

To this documented opinion, Theall adds this more personal barb:

> Wolfe positioned McLuhan as the contemporary Freud ... McLuhan's rise was through conscious manipulation of the very instruments ... [he] had moralistically criticized in *The Mechanical Bride*.[10]

To this and other criticisms, McLuhan would probably have retorted his customary quip: "As for critics, don't even bother to ignore them."[11]

However, in spite of what must have already been a decade of experience with corporate culture, it is hard to imagine McLuhan as a slick and conniving operator. Witness the exchange that occurred in New York in May, 1965. It is recounted by Tom Wolfe in the famous article, "What If He Is Right?"[12]

Howard Luck Gossage has taken a suite at New York's Lombardy Hotel. Marshall McLuhan is with him. A manager from one of the United States' largest packing corporations calls for McLuhan. The corporation is interested in retaining him for a three-day series of talks — one per day — to be given to their senior management team. The manager asks how much McLuhan would charge for such an outing.

My detractors work night and day to advance my reputation. It is impossible to buy so invaluable a service!

Letters of Marshall McLuhan, 1970

While the manager waits on the line, McLuhan explains the situation to Gossage.

Gossage asks McLuhan how much he normally charges for a single lecture. McLuhan replies that his normal fee is five hundred dollars. Gossage responds: "Tell him a hundred thousand." McLuhan appears aghast at the suggestion. Gossage relents. "Oh, all right. Tell him fifty thousand."

With trepidation, McLuhan returns to the manager and relates his new price. It is the manager's turn to be aghast. He sputters that the fee is somewhat higher than they had expected for such an engagement. He then goes on to explain that the material they would want McLuhan to use would not have to be new, and that his entire tenure would amount to only three lectures.

Feigning a new understanding, McLuhan lowers his price. "Oh — well then, twenty-five thousand," says the professor. An agreement is quickly reached, much to the relief of the man from the packaging company.

McLuhan turns to Gossage, somewhat bewildered at the transaction. But Gossage is already carried away with gales of laughter and eyes aglow at the possibilities. At that instant, Gossage knew, even though McLuhan did not, that this shy, guileless English professor from Canada would suddenly emerge as a celebrity on the world stage, one of the most famous people Canada would ever produce.

Tom Wolfe, one of the greatest among the living writers of America, was also one of the earliest public figures to recognize McLuhan's genius and to promote it. He said:

> I pay attention to every one of Marshall's insights, no matter how implausible they seem at the time, because he has been proven right over and over again. ... His stock in the world will return as people look back with a little more detachment. The insights, the aphorisms, the sayings, have forced people to re-interpret the world they live in.[13]

Wolfe seems to allude to what was a kind of "rise and fall" story in McLuhan's fame. We could add "rise and fall and rise again." Indeed, there is a revival of McLuhan today after a couple of decades of neglect. When people talk about the "Global Village" or the bias of media today, McLuhan's name is often invoked as if to support a claim or a statement by the principal authority behind it. However, there was a great dip in McLuhan's reputation, especially during the 1970s and 1980s. This is easy to understand: McLuhan was associated with the openness and the freedom of the "Affluent Society" of the middle and late 1960s. His perception of contemporary culture was that of a "brave new world," in the bloom of youthful innocence and in full and limitless expansion, quite unaware of its tragic past — the Great Depression and World War Two. However, during the early 1970s, after what seemed to be irrepressible waves of inflation, a rapid succession of recessions brought down the boundless optimism of the "Affluent Society" and with it the relevance of McLuhan.

McLuhan perhaps best expresses his own perception of his "rise and fall" in a letter to Marshall Fishwick, dated August 1, 1974:

His perception of contemporary culture was that of a "brave new world," in the bloom of youthful innocence, quite unaware of its tragic past.

Apropos my sudden prominence in the 60's, it happened with the dropout TV generation who were happy to discover the rage which my stuff produced in the academic bosom and to associate themselves with me on that account. Now that the TV generation is squaring up again, they no longer feel the same satisfaction in zapping the establishment via McLuhan.[14]

Perhaps McLuhan's fall also had something to do with the rising influence of computers bringing in a new generation of thinking — and lifestyles from hippies to yuppies — with sharp minds and serious cost-benefit analyses. McLuhan was far too fuzzy for the computer generation.

Business as an Art Form

McLuhan's fuzziness served other purposes. John Cage, among the most important — and insightful — composers of the twentieth century, in answer to the question about how McLuhan had influenced his thinking, said:

I am today indebted to McLuhan as I ever was. He was a creative critic, probably the only one there ever was. His observations of art, media, society, in some cases corroborated the independent actions of artists, in other cases suggested what the next ones might rightly be.[15]

Indeed, McLuhan was very close to the art world, not so much as a consumer for his own enjoyment, but as an explorer for his personal instruction.

He also extended the notion of art: He saw art where others would see merely business, politics and education. McLuhan recognized as artist, any person capable of "integral perception," the model for understanding in any field. He would say that if you wanted to understand what was going on, you would first ask the artist, then the business person because both had a vested interest in observation and understanding for their survival. Both the artist and the business person are hunters.

McLuhan's motivation to pay attention to business was one of genuine appreciation for what he could learn about his own time by being exposed to corporate culture. Business was a source of insights for McLuhan almost to the same extent as art. He looked upon businesses the way he looked at art forms, that is, as different arrays of constraints and possibilities that generated different, but highly discernible, patterns depending on their contexts.

Indeed, for McLuhan, pattern recognition is where literary criticism and the business world began to connect. It happened in three steps: First, he was trained as a young student of literature to examine the evidence of texts and, with the help of sophisticated methods, to discover their deeper meanings. He was especially good at a form of New Criticism which privileged the study of effects over that of causes. The whole idea was to know the work of art by what it could do or was intended to do to the consumer rather than by trying to define the work itself. The New Critics would try to find out the potential effects of the poem rather than the meaning of the text. McLuhan simply transferred that skill to public advertisements.

Second, as a young teacher in the U.S., McLuhan found out that his students didn't have a clue about literature, and that he didn't have a clue about them. He wondered why they had absolutely no interest in Mathew Arnold or Edmund Burke, or even Shakespeare. He asked himself what could possibly shape the thoughts, feelings and tastes of his students. He began to consider that perhaps "Burke is feeble stuff to pit against Bogart."[16] McLuhan recounts to Gerald Stearn his first experience as a teacher:

The artist is the man in any field, scientific or humanistic, who grasps the implications of his actions and of new knowledge in his own time. Understanding Media, 1964

In 1936, when I arrived at Wisconsin, I confronted classes of freshmen and I suddenly realized that I was incapable of understanding them. I felt an urgent need to study their popular culture: advertising, games, movies. It was pedagogy, part of my teaching program. To meet them on their grounds was my strategy in pedagogy: the world of pop culture.[17]

Finally, he focused his attention on advertising as one of the main supporters of popular culture and common mindset.

Advertising was a very convenient form of approach. I used advertising in the [Mechanical] Bride because of legal considerations – no permissions were needed. Otherwise I would have used picture stories of any sort from movies, magazines, anywhere.[18]

Hardly back from England, where advertising in the pre-war era had little hold over the popular imagination, McLuhan readily saw a key difference in how his young North American students reacted to what became known as "popular culture." Ten years after, in the late 1940s and early 1950s, he would likewise witness and assess the effects of the early stirrings of television.

This early work led him to explore what he called the "folklore of industrial man,"[19] to "immunize the student against his environment,"[20] as he put it. At the time, his attitude was moralistic and generally unsupportive of business practices. However, even in the published preface of this first book, he observed that, "the time for anger and protest is in the early stages of a new process. The present stage is extremely advanced. Moreover, it is full, not only of destructiveness but also of promises of rich new developments to which moral indignation is a very poor guide."[21]

The Mechanical Bride was the first of two books that find McLuhan studying advertisements as if they were poems. It addressed billboards, newspapers, magazines and other print-based ads. Twenty years later, the second book, *Culture Is Our Business*, is an updated look at advertising that had since been significantly affected and influenced by television. McLuhan observed that:

…we are swiftly moving at present from an era when business was our culture into an era when culture will be our business. … As the new media unfold their powers the entertainment industries swallow

> ⋰ The job of art is not to store moments of experience but to explore environments that are otherwise invisible. McLuhan Hot & Cool, 1967

more and more of the old business culture. The movie industry is thus an inseparable portion of the advertising industry in providing the necessary drama of consumption, in which the ads merely provide the news.[22]

The book tackles the kind of economy that develops under the new dominance of television. Abandoning the moral high ground, McLuhan also let go of the need to explain. Instead of a secure narrative thread to support a theory or a point-of-view, all he provides the reader is a series of juxtaposed ads, quotations, quips and comments. This is the "mosaic" method for which McLuhan found justification in the layout of any newspaper with its juxtaposed ads, news and glosses without necessary connections between any, as he tells Louis Forsdale in a casual, but carefully recorded, conversation in 1966:

McLuhan also let go of the need to explain. All he provides the reader is a series of juxtaposed ads, quotations, quips and comments.

> This, by the way, is what happens to your newspaper under telegraph conditions. At the speed of light, there are no connections in the news. Everything is apposed, or juxtaposed minus connections. There are no connections in the news, they're just mosaic. At the speed of light you have a mosaic under one dateline and no connections.[23]

Whatever the justification, the result does not make for easy reading. It is the reader's job to draw the connections and derive the insights. Depending on how one feels that day, *Culture Is Our Business* will occasion wonderful insights, or nothing at all.

McLuhan's mind functioned like the Web. He would associate, link, relate and draw analogies between ideas, observations and notions as far apart as satellites, the genetic code and the comic strip, *Li'l Abner*. And he would do it with casual aplomb, not bothering to draw out the connections per se. In fact, he would bristle at the word "connection." He thought that connectivity, just like theory, was hopelessly "visual," that is, a one-dimensional and outmoded strategy to understand anything. In McLuhan's opinion, seemingly unrelated things could yield an insight once they were brought in vicinity of each other. In his writing, he was fond of using the technique of collage and juxtaposition, sometimes including pictures and designs, not to illustrate a point but merely to bring out new ones from the reader.

McLuhan's really great book, *Understanding Media*, becomes increasingly accessible with each subsequent reading. McLuhan's approach to each individual medium is discursive, attentive, systematic and immensely learned without pretence. Reading this book, you feel that you share with McLuhan the sense that you are "in the know" even though this book is already forty years old. The chapters that are most directly useful for business people in *Understanding Media* are those on Clocks, on Money — The Poor Man's Credit Card and on Automation. They provide a kind of review of the cultural and technological underpinnings of all the major sectors of industry, endowed with an absolute certitude about precisely what kind of business each industry is actually in. This is something that few managers understand about their own enterprises, and an issue we examine in later chapters of this book.

> He thought that connectivity, just like theory, was hopelessly "visual," that is, a one-sided and outmoded strategy to understand anything.

McLuhan and the Economy

If few business people made much sense of *Culture Is Our Business*, even fewer found easy access to the ocean of meaning that is contained in *Take Today: The Executive as Dropout*, the least talked-about and last business book McLuhan helped to write. There is a significant progression from *Culture Is Our Business* to *Take Today* — which appeared two years later. The first is based on the concerns of advertisers, while the latter is a much more comprehensive attempt at understanding the economy of a world transformed by electricity. *Take Today* is also the only book that McLuhan addressed specifically to managers and business executives. It is full of original and useful ideas mired in wordplay, sidetracks and happenstance gibberish. *Take Today* identifies three dominant trends that affect not only businesses and the economy, but also social and political developments:

1. **A general trend to decentralization.** Thanks to improved communications and the "speed of light," distance in many instances is overcome and removed as an obstacle. You can conduct business anywhere. The Internet and mobility afforded by portable, wireless devices today potentially carry

this trend to the extreme, enabling previously unimagined possibilities. Everything is made available to everyone everywhere, allowing the ultimate deterritorialization that is the virtual.[24]

2. **A general shift from hardware to software.** Over twenty years before Nicholas Negroponte, McLuhan had foreseen that technology and culture would go from "atoms to bits" because he knew that the effect of electricity was to dematerialize the support systems of human communication. We see this shift continuing today in the digitization and the virtualization of culture.[25]

3. **A general morphing of people's jobs into roles and role-playing.** This is the most original trend identified by McLuhan and his co-author, Barrington Nevitt, and the one that applies most directly to managers today. It is also a very useful object of meditation for managers who would like to instill more entrepreneurship among their staff.[26]

While these themes are now familiar to today's managers and executives, it is remarkable to contemplate that McLuhan made these observations over thirty years ago! In fact, the inspiration for the practical research that resulted in this book originally came from this realization and the subsequent question: What would McLuhan predict if he were able to look at our world today and think about what is happening right now?

McLuhan with Managers

Even in the late 1970s, McLuhan would routinely receive three and more invitations a day from all parts of the world. Derrick de Kerckhove, who speaks French and Italian, was occasionally on call at the Centre for Culture and Technology to negotiate telephone exchanges with European organizations. Once in 1972, expecting yet another insistent call from a big Italian media concern, he asked McLuhan how to handle the next request: "Ask $5,000," said McLuhan. Now, in 1972, $5,000 had the buying power of approximately $25,000 today. This was McLuhan's fencing-off strategy, but it didn't always work. This sum discouraged many, but not all callers, and McLuhan would sometimes find himself trapped by his own ploy.[27]

And when he got there, how would his audience receive him? His first big-ticket conferences were a series of seminars with General Electric that began in 1960 at their Management Center near New York City. GE's private school, intended for the edification of the higher echelons of the business community, was the first of its kind. The GE school was inspired by Peter Drucker, to this day one of the most revered management consultants and theorists, and a long-time friend and occasional supporter of McLuhan.

What would McLuhan predict if he were able to look at our world today and think about what is happening right now?

Certain that the intensified application of intellect to business would result in a brave new world, McLuhan perceived nothing but exciting possibilities in his work with the executives of General Electric. For the most part the executives seemed to respond well to his enthusiasm. Occasionally, such as in the washroom between lectures ... some of the men [would be heard] grumbling about McLuhan's far-out ideas.[28]

On another occasion, in 1966, after McLuhan's speech at the Laurentian Conference, then Canada's most prestigious annual event for senior business executives, and at which Drucker was also present, one of the attendants was heard saying:

A few years ago, he'd have been kicked out bodily. But business has changed. You've got younger, more aware men at the helm. I don't pretend to understand him but I want him around just in case he's right.[29]

Dean Walker, a staff writer for *Executive*, a Canadian business magazine, points out that McLuhan simultaneously enthralled and frustrated his business audiences:

He worries executives who are fitfully aware that he is intriguing on subjects they feel should concern them. They find it hard to evaluate him or come to grips with what he says ... He is the sort of person they might normally ignore but they are not sure they can because he talks about media, communications, advertising, and social patterns.[30]

In 1968, addressing executives from IBM, McLuhan again faced incredulity from his audience. Arthur Porter, one of Canada's pioneers of Operations Research and one of the persons at the University of Toronto who was responsible for the creation of the Centre for Culture and Technology, recalls this reaction from IBM executives in 1968:

> Marshall was telling them [a dozen of IBM's divisional directors] about a computer for every home, no need to visit the grocery... Two of them said to me after lunch, "We haven't heard of anything as crazy as that!" Marshall was talking about the personal computer a dozen years before they thought of it. Here was a professor of English more than a decade ahead of the technical people in computer evolution.[31]

It is obvious that while McLuhan enjoyed a friendly and humorous rapport with managers and executives, his speaking style was not any more accessible than was his writing style in *Take Today* or *Culture Is Our Business*. Nonetheless, as his predictions and creative thinking so eloquently demonstrate, understanding his approach to thinking about the challenges of business is clearly worth the investment of time and effort. Our goal in the pages ahead is to make McLuhan's thinking tools not only accessible but practical and useful to managers and executives today.

2. What haven't you noticed lately?

"There is no single approach to this task, and no single observation or idea that can solve so complex a problem in changing human perception."

—Understanding Media, 1964

Put down this book, just for a moment or two, and glance around. Are you in a familiar environment? In your study? Your office? Your living room? A departure lounge or on board an aircraft? Can you close your eyes and describe your surroundings? If you are in a well-known setting, your description will undoubtedly include features you have seen hundreds, or perhaps thousands of times before. Stimuli normally captured by our senses will blend into a "scape" — soundscape, sightscape, smellscape — easily filtered by the brain, and for the most part, ignored.

Now put the book down once more, and look for something new, something you haven't noticed lately. Notice what your mind does with this new awareness, this different perception of familiar surroundings. If you are like most people, your mental activity has just stepped up a notch. You may ask yourself a question: "How did that get here?" "Why is this out of place?" You may be moved to action: "I've got to take care of that." "I must put that away." Or, you may have the common realization: "I've never noticed that before!"

"What haven't you noticed lately?" is, in itself, an absurd question. Attempting to answer it presents an interesting paradox: If you can actually supply an answer — "I haven't noticed *this* before" — you have, in fact, noticed it! As you may have guessed, discovering an answer is not the true purpose of the question. Rather, it is the pursuit — the process of discovering the answer — and the ensuing mental activity that brings value to the question.

Dealing with the pursuit and the process of discovery — in reality, making sense of a conundrum — is quintessentially McLuhanesque. It is a "probe," an investigation specifically designed not merely for the purpose of noticing something new, but for the new thoughts the noticing engenders. These new thoughts will provoke more questions, more probing, more curiosity, more investigation, more playing and perhaps most important, more thinking. In search of the unnoticed, a person gains new perception and awareness about the present environment, surroundings and conditions.

In a business environment, managers seldom have difficulty with familiar and comfortable surroundings — business as usual, steady production, healthy revenue, growing profit, happy customers, competitors held at bay. When the surroundings become less familiar and friendly, managers become worried and seek quick solutions to restore the status quo. Immediate corrective action is frequently demanded by impatient shareholders and boards of directors. The imperative is to do anything, so long as it is quick and will provide some symptomatic relief, before issuing the next quarterly results. As a result, there is precious little time to search for root causes and determine an appropriate path to a sustainable solution. There is also no time to consider possible secondary and tertiary effects that may result from imposing quick action. And most certainly, there is no time to notice that which has not been noticed lately.

It seems that all a manager needs these days is a way of predicting the future. If the manager, facing a myriad of challenges, were merely able to predict the outcomes of actions and the future effects of decisions taken now, all else would unfold as it should. For example, what if someone could have considered the nature of radio and television from the 1950s through the 1970s, and subsequently predicted the extension of such instantaneous communication into today's Internet? What if he or she could have predicted the effects of instantaneous communications on business, culture and society in general? And, what if business actually heeded those predictions and used them to tactical or strategic advantage?

Now, imagine if that someone were available to sit with business managers today. Together, they would consider difficult and challenging problems and apply the same thinking tools and techniques that were used to predict the effects of an embryonic Internet, as Marshall McLuhan did over thirty years ago.

Perception 101 Figure and Ground

At the beginning of this chapter, we proposed a simple exercise in perception: Notice something new or different in a familiar surrounding, something you haven't noticed lately. In one sense, a very familiar environment is quite homogeneous — nothing in particular stands out as unique or worthy of special notice. If you were able to notice something new or distinct, you actually observed a *figure* — the new — against its *ground* — the familiar. In this instance what made the observed item or situation new is precisely the familiarity of the rest. It was the particular familiarity with your surroundings that

What made the observed item new is precisely the familiarity of the rest.

provided the context within which "what you haven't noticed lately" existed and had meaning as a distinct entity.

McLuhan told us that "nothing has its meaning alone."[1] Something may exist in isolation, but its meaning — and by extension, its value — is derived solely as a function of the context or environment in which it exists. There are many examples of this.

The Co-Op Student

Consider a student with limited job-related programming skills. Taken as a *figure* in isolation, no judgement can be made about the student, as there is no context against which the attributes of the student can be measured. Furthermore, the relevance of the student's attributes to the particular situation cannot even be determined, since we have provided no pertinent information. In other words, a *figure* out of context, in isolation, has no meaning.

Now take a moment and contemplate the *figure* of the student cast against the following work scenarios as *ground*:

- The student is the only programmer set to work on a business-critical production application by a penny-pinching company that could otherwise afford to pay for experience.

- The student is hired by a university research project to work on experimental development related to his or her studies.

- The student is a close relative of the company's president.

- The student is a close relative of the company's largest customer's president.

- The student is part of a large development team working on a business-critical production application. She has been hired by a company that tends to recruit full-time employees from among prior interns.

Each scenario provokes a distinct managerial reaction: positive, negative or neutral. In each, the student did not change but the context did. In changing the *ground*, the advisability of the decision to place the student in the particular employment situation also changed from one scenario to the next. In other words, our perception of the situation changed by virtue of the context. This example is deliberately contrived. However, there are non-trivial instances in business that may give the thinking manager pause.

Customer Relationship Management

For many companies, the euphemistically named "Customer Relationship Management" (CRM) in fact represents retooled business processes, often implemented as expensive and large — some may say cumbersome — computer systems. Among the nominal objectives of such systems are the rather ambitious but vague notions of "taking control of the customer relationship" by maintaining a central repository of all recorded interactions; understanding the profitability of any given customer — and presumably redeploying resources away from those found to be unprofitable; and, of course, increasing both sales to, and the "share" of total expenditures by, any particular customer.

At face value, these stated goals are laudable. After all, what manager would not want to increase sales to a well-managed customer, particularly when that customer has been proven to be profitable? Clearly, the benefits of such processes are so obvious that any manager would be foolish not to embark on the good ship CRM. They would have been just as foolish not to have embarked on its sister ships BPR and TQM — Business Process Re-engineering and Total Quality Management — before that. However, like so many prior acronymic initiatives, the benefits are not always without significant long-term consequences.

Given the cost — financial as well as human — of any of these initiatives, how could management avoid what, in many instances, has proven to be a massive mistake? The perceptive manager would consider the CRM initiative as the *figure*, to be cast against an appropriate *ground* that would supply the context, and thereby provide meaning. An appropriate *ground* in this case may well be the company's customer base itself.

Like so many acronymic initiatives, the benefits are not always without significant long-term consequences.

In contemplating the relationship between the initiative and the customers — between *figure* and *ground* — the manager may be moved to question whether the CRM processes and system are exclusively introspective. That is, does all the information collected and managed by the system ultimately focus on what the customers do for the company — revenue, profit, product mix, share of business and so forth? Is there any way of understanding what customers do outside of the direct company relationship, like buying from other companies or partnering with other customers? Are there any system components that collect comparable information on what the company does for the customers — measurements of satisfaction or outcomes? If so, are there standard, well-integrated ways of comparing aspects of *figure* against the *ground* — individual customer profitability versus that customer's satisfaction, for instance?

CRM systems often result in segmentation and fragmenting of one's customers — separating those that are currently profitable from those that are not. How does a manager predict which "non-productive" customer today will become tomorrow's showcase for a new strategic initiative? Clearly there must be at least a second *ground* of consideration introduced. This leaves one to wonder, "Are there any other important contexts that may yet be hidden in our pursuit of Customer Relationship?"

The *figure* standing alone, out of context, has no meaning. Or, at least, it has no meaning with respect to any measure of relevance by which a manager can fairly judge its value to, or for, the enterprise. Conversely, when *figure* fades into *ground*, the *ground*, now devoid of *figure*, blurs because it is all background. The effect on a manager is soporific and dulling. It is a vehicle for "anti-awareness," with potentially devastating effects on a business.

Fading *Figure*: the Implosion of TNT

The crash of the technology and telecom sectors of the economy, and those companies that supplied them, is perhaps a sobering example of what happens when *ground* stands alone, without *figure*. After many decades of slow but sure growth from blue chip companies, the dramatic increase in demand for Internet-fuelled technology through the latter half of the 1990s resulted in tremendous growth in the technology and telecom sectors. Companies that supplied the basic components and infrastructure for the so-called new economy experienced unprecedented year-over-year growth in revenue, profit and production capacity. When set against the *ground* of old-economy earnings growth and expectations, the new economic *figure* displayed itself in high relief.

Success begot a strange combination of complacency and arrogance among the tech and telecom — let's call them TNT for short — business leaders. Unprecedented expansion in earnings growth became the expected norm among financial analysts and investors alike. A company reporting year-over-year growth in profits was contrarily punished with a sell-off of its stock if the rate of growth was not sufficiently large. Conversely, TNT companies with no earnings whatsoever were rewarded with astronomical forward earnings multiples — the factor by which projected future earnings, or net profit, is multiplied to obtain the current stock price. The expectation of never-ending demand fuelled unrestrained building of capacity, financed by ever-inflating market valuations and supposedly synergistic mergers or acquisitions.

Of course, the inevitable happened: TNT imploded. Perhaps the only thing that was surprising in the collapse of this sector was that its leaders were surprised. Intelligent men and women at the pinnacle of their careers, unanimously hailed as business visionaries, were all asleep at the switch, so to speak.

What went wrong?

Simply put, *figure* was allowed to fade into *ground*. The resultant blur induced the business version of "highway hypnosis." What once stood prominently as *figure* — unprecedented growth in demand, revenue and profits driven by new and original business concepts — became the context. As there was no "context for the context," the strategists of most major TNT corporations could easily ignore the warnings of naysayers for whom a new *figure/ground* combination was frighteningly obvious. In retrospect, with the time-distanced ability to discern what was hidden *ground*, it is now obvious to all of us, including the strategists.

What happens when *figure* and *ground* "flip," swapping positions with each other in a manager's mind? That is, what is the risk to mana-gerial judgement and decision making if the context of a given business situation is taken from the *figure*, rather than being established by the *ground*? Consider the following example.

As we do more with less, we invent by design. Take Today: The Executive as Dropout, 1972

Figure/Ground Hoedown

Among many TNT companies, it had become a management cliché for a professor from a prominent and respected university to become the Chief Technology Officer. The professor, in the role of senior manager, leads the research and development efforts, directs the product engineering and is responsible for the technical infrastructure through which products and services are delivered.

"Professor Cito" is the *figure* that we can cast against the *ground* to judge the advisability of such an arrangement. If the company is indeed a high-technology company, that is, one heavily involved in original, advanced research and development, the appointment of the professor as CTO is reasonable. The focus of the company is the development of new and innovative intellectual property. The relationship between Professor Cito and high-tech company — *figure* and *ground* — makes sense.

However, what if the company is a "medium technology" company? By this we mean a company that uses known technologies to provide products and deliver services. In this case, the technical emphasis is not on advanced research and development, but rather on production operations, reliability, scalability, fault tolerance, maintainability and similar considerations. Is a research-oriented professor the best one to lead the technology and engineering efforts for this company?

Clearly, unless the professor has prior, relevant industry experience, his role in the medium-tech company will be instructive — for him. In all likelihood, Professor Cito will apply his research-oriented knowledge and experience to direct the company's technical architecture, product development and delivery infrastructure. Here, the technical context is being set not by the company's needs but rather by the professor's own academic and research background. From our McLuhanistic perspective, *figure* and *ground* — professor and company — have changed places. As the relationship between *figure* and *ground* is inverted, decisions made on the basis of the inverted meaning — the professor's needs rather than the company's setting the context — may appear somewhat bizarre to the casual observer. The outsider has the benefit of observing from a more objective and appropriate *ground*.

In this practical example, the outcome is that neither the company's nor the professor's best interests are served. Professor Cito finds himself in unfamiliar territory, attempting to manage outside of his skills and expertise. The company is left with systems that are developed in a context of experimental research and are anything but robust and production-ready. Customers are unwittingly exposed to systems that may be feature-rich, but almost certainly not production-grade. *Figure* switching places with *ground*, again clouds perception, leading to poor decisions.

The outsider has the benefit of observing from a more objective and appropriate *ground*.

Insight and Awareness 101 The Medium and the Message

"The Medium is the Message" is undoubtedly the singular, most well known of the multitude of Marshall McLuhan's sayings. And, it is most assuredly among the most misunderstood. Like Albert Einstein's famous relativity equation, $E = mc^2$, few people who have heard the McLuhan Equation, Medium = Message, understand what it means, its implications and its consequences.

To most people, the media are information channels, most commonly the press, television, radio and the Internet. The message of a medium is most often mistaken as the information content it conveys. From McLuhan's perspective, our conventional examples of media are for the most part correct, but not for the reasons we would immediately guess. As for our understanding of message, the popular view could not be further from what McLuhan had in mind.

In McLuhan's world a *Medium* is anything that extends our mind, body or senses. It could be a new technology or gadget. It could be a new process. An idea or original, creative work is a Medium. Anything we create or build, anything we conceive, any expression of humankind is a McLuhanesque Medium. Media — more than one Medium — can be concrete and tangible or they may be abstract and intangible.

Examples are easy to find, and indeed, Marshall McLuhan offered them. Clothing is an extension of our skin. The motorcycle is an extension of the bicycle, which itself extends our leg and foot. The microphone and radio are both extensions of our voice. What we conventionally conceive of as the media — the press, radio, television, and so forth — are examples of McLuhan's perception of Media, extending our ears and eyes to the world, expanding the reach of voices and the influence of ideas.

Company = Medium

A company or corporation is a Medium. It extends our ability to work, either with muscle power or brain power, beyond that of an individual. We speak of a corporation "extending its reach" across the country or around the world. This, of course, is the metaphorical extension of our arms and hands. The term "reach" in this context could easily apply to ideas, influence, intellectual property and political points of view as well, extending the capacity of the human brain and mind. It has been said, for example, that the spread of capitalism and democracy could not have progressed so rapidly without major multi-national corporations playing their roles so well.

Among strategy consultants, and in corporate executive suites, we speak of a corporation's "vision" — an extension of the sense of sight. Companies have been issuing statements of late, addressing their ability or inability to see their future financial path, using terms such as "visibility" — or the lack thereof — of upcoming fiscal results. Like many of us, companies are often sensitive to local culture and mores. McDonald's in India, for example, has taken to not serving beef in deference to Hindu customs; KFC in Israel prepares Kosher Fried Chicken. These are examples of company-as-Medium extending the human sense of hearing as it "listens to its local customers" and quite literally, extending taste and smell also — although, in some cases, there is no accounting for taste. Legally, corporations are considered persons. From the perspective of a McLuhanesque Medium, a corporation is very much the extension of a person.

> A McLuhanesque perspective helps us make sense of the confusing mass of information with which we all have to deal.

For those who have recently entered McLuhan's world, this new notion of Media may be somewhat perplexing, confusing and perhaps disorienting. Relax. It gets easier over time. And in fact, a McLuhanesque perspective helps us make sense of the confusing and perplexing mass of information with which we all regularly have to deal.

Information Overload

Before stepping into the world as perceived by McLuhan, our conventional view has been that media were simply channels for conveying information. Information comes from outside of our direct sensory experience, to the inside of our minds. For example, when we read about an event in the press, we do not experience it directly. Seeing fireworks on television is distinctly different than feeling the compression of the explosion and marvelling at the night sky lit with a multitude of colours. We often view the bombardment of multiple media as just that — multiple incessant channels of information that inundate us. To be sure, the flood of information is often extreme; some even feel compelled to turn it off. Unplug the television! Turn on the answering machine and ignore the messages! Throw away the cell phone! Turn off the computer! It's little wonder that so many people identify with the popular television and advertising image of computers being thrown from high-rise office windows.

Others cope by simply casting the flow of information to the McLuhanesque *ground*, considering it — or rather, not considering it at all — as the blur it appears to be. The torrent of information takes on the characteristics of wallpaper, providing merely a backdrop for modern life that is easily ignored. This typifies information overload, the bane of modern business managers and our modern, western society in general.

Why does information overload happen? The easy response may be that we simply have too much exposure to the media. But McLuhan reminds us that we are literally surrounded by Media — everything we have created, fabricated or conceived (every idea, every work of art, music and literature, our homes, our companies, our institutions) they are all Media. Clearly "too much Media" is not the root of our feelings of frustration, desperation and despair. Rather, we have become too enamoured with, focused on and vested in information — the content of the Media. Why do you think it's called *information* overload in the first place?

McLuhan has some advice on what to do with the content. However, before we get to that, knowing that Message does not equal content is fundamental to understanding the McLuhan Equation, the Medium is the Message. Mistaking Medium as merely a conveyance of content limits our thinking, causing us to ignore the true nature of the Medium. In one sense, the Message is anything and everything but the content!

> **Mistaking Medium as merely a conveyance of content limits our thinking, causing us to ignore its true nature.**

In our developing new perspective on the world, the Message of a Medium is the resultant "change of scale, pace or pattern"[2] that a Medium causes in ourselves, in society or in a culture. This is clearly distinct from the content of the Medium. This seemingly obscure view is based on the notion that the information itself is not necessarily what is important to understand or appreciate the nature, power and potential of the Medium. The Medium's ability to effect change is what is important to realize and understand. Consider one of McLuhan's favourite examples: television.

We Now Pause for a *Message* from Our Television

It is now well accepted that investigative journalism is an effective tool that checks the behaviour of politicians and corporations. For television, *60 Minutes*, the news magazine broadcast weekly on the CBS network, is among the most well known of this genre. In 1996, a *60 Minutes* producer received secret, internal information from Jeffrey Wigand, a former Vice-President for Research and Development with the Brown and Williamson tobacco company. The publicity about the story, the company's attempts to suppress it and subsequent public disclosure of the secret information ultimately led to huge financial payments by Brown and Williamson, and the other American tobacco companies, to settle litigation in many states. As part of the settlement, fundamental changes have been effected in the behaviour of these corporations with regard to marketing tobacco products, and perhaps as well, in the opinions of some of the management as to the addictive nature of their products.[3]

We could easily conclude that without the information content of the television Medium, none of these changes would have occurred. While this is true, the content addresses this specific instance of "David and Goliaths" — Wigand

and the Tobacco Industry — focusing on the importance of the content alone would require us to examine each of an infinite number of instances to understand the Medium of television. Instead, by contemplating the Message, that is, the resultant change in scale, pace or pattern caused by television, we can begin to understand the true nature of the Medium. In this instance, we can see that television has the capacity to effect significant behavioural change in powerful and influential monolithic entities by extending vision, hearing and the ability to share even more powerful and influential ideas.

By 1996 we already knew this, although it took between one and two decades from the invention of television for us to fully get the picture. Most people who have been alive since the 1960s have experienced television's profound effects on politics, international diplomacy and the nature of war, for example. Today, television's ability to effect change has been seconded by many organizations that have twisted the "normal" dynamics of its potential. Political candidates are created for television and wars are staged for the benefit of the six o'clock news — without having to wait for "film at eleven." International diplomacy among governments and corporations are choreographed for the benefit of insatiable all-news networks, complete with the now *de rigueur* demonstrations and concomitant police overreaction.

To be sure, the tragedy of September 11, 2001, in which two hijacked commercial jetliners were deliberately flown into the Twin Towers of the World Trade Center in New York City, starkly highlights television's effect. For the first time in history, television was used to attract millions of viewers to witness a previously unimaginable act of terrorism live, as it happened.

One effect of television is to bring the outside world into our homes. By staging the attack as they did, the terrorist hijackers directly attacked not only the occupants of the Twin Towers, but 300 million Americans too. Television was "flipped" into a weapon of mass destruction.

McLuhan noted that, "We shape our tools and thereafter our tools shape us."[5] As we create a new Medium, its Message is the consequential changes in the nature, pace and scope of our interactions and activities. By virtue of these changes, we are changed as we react to the new

We shape our tools and thereafter our tools shape us. Understanding Media, MIT Press Edition, 1994

pace or scale. The changes induced by the terrorist attack on TV are only now becoming clear.

Television reports a demonstration. The demonstrators realize that the existence of television changes the scale of their ability to transmit their grievances, from a local audience to a global one. As a result, when news cameras appear, so too do the demonstrators. Once the requisite film clip is captured, both the camera crew and the demonstrators return home. Further, because television is such an intimate experience — a wide field of view contained in a relatively small box, centred in one's living room — ten people shouting with raised fists can be made to seem like a massive mob.

Feedforward

"… and thereafter our tools shape us." The key to understanding a Medium, is to understand its effects in totality. As we — the collective "we" of a business, a market, a target demographic, a society or culture — experience these effects, we cannot help but be changed by them. As our perspective changes, so does the *ground* that provides a context for the Medium. As the context changes, the Medium is subsequently affected, and around it goes. Our reaction to the anticipation of this is the McLuhanesque notion of "feedforward."

It is too simple to call feedforward a never-ending cycle, because it is not a cycle. Rather, it is a network of effects — Messages upon Messages interacting with one another causing a dynamic, ever-shifting *ground*. The *ground* remakes itself every minute of every day, continually shifting the context, and the Messages, of our Media. There is little wonder why, with our insatiable hunger for information and content superimposed on Media dynamics, our world of instantaneous communication has become confusing, ambiguous and uncertain.

Today, regardless of the uncertainty, business cannot afford to wait between one and two decades to comprehend the nature of Media that are being created at an ever-accelerating pace. We cannot rely on years of experience with a particular Medium and the ability to sufficiently filter the content so that the more general, higher-level effects become obvious. This is particularly true if the Medium under consideration is a new product about to launch or a new subsidiary ready to spin off. In addition, knowing that the changes caused by the new Medium will in turn change our behaviour and reactions, it is crucial to be able to fully understand the complete Message of the Medium.

Internet = Medium = Message

Take, for example, the Internet as an extension of our bodies and minds. We speak of "virtual presence" and online communities. E-mail extends our speech; Web pages extend our thoughts and creativity. Web cams extend our eyes; streaming audio media, our ears. Through online chat and instant messaging, the Internet extends conversation and the immediacy — and occasionally intimacy — of physical presence. The Internet is a McLuhan Medium.

The Internet has also caused significant changes in the scale, pace and patterns of our interactions — both business and personal — with other people. We are able to easily conduct affairs with others in distant locales in an unprecedented fashion. This has enabled businesses to open new markets without first establishing a physical presence, eliminating prior impediments of time (zones) and (geographical) space. The change in the velocity of information has enabled new modes of doing business that formerly were hampered by — or in some cases relied on — the time lag of information flow. Such an immediate availability of information, for example, caused a fundamental change in the way people invested in financial markets. It caused upheavals in the way business investment occurred, and the expectations imposed on those businesses. It forced changes in financial disclosure rules and improved fairness for smaller investors.

In other cases, instantaneous information allowed for significant improvements in the flow of goods and services as supply chains could be better managed. This, in turn, has affected expectations of producers, suppliers and consumers with respect to product availability, inventory control and price. The Internet clearly is a McLuhan Message.

Whether the Medium is a concept or product, its significance is equal to the change it effects.

The Medium IS the Message.

The McLuhan Equation means that the change effected by a Medium is precisely equal to the Medium itself, and vice versa. Whether the Medium is a concept or a product, its meaning and significance are equal to the change it effects. Thus the measure of a Medium — say, the effectiveness of a new product — can be known by knowing the extent and magnitude of its effects. Will the product be great? Is a new technology truly significant? Will an advertising campaign be effective? Is this business strategy sufficient? Will the organizational change allow us to accomplish our goals? All of these questions ask about the measure of the Medium — a product, a technology, an ad campaign, a business strategy, a shuffling of the "org chart." To answer these questions, or at least gain some awareness of what the answers may be, you must examine the Media's respective Messages to determine magnitude, scope, extent, secondary effects and so forth. This examination often provides new and sometimes startling insights that will guide your decision making with new awareness and clarity.

Properly identifying and understanding a Medium, and in particular a new or evolving Medium, is crucial. Assuming it would be possible, comprehending the Message with complete clarity is the key to successfully proceeding with introducing or using the new Medium. Consider some examples noted by McLuhan in 1964.

- By examining the effects of its products on its customers' operations, IBM discovered it was not in the business of making office equipment or business machines, but in the business of processing information.

- Conversely, General Electric believed that it was in the electric light bulb and lighting systems business. It had not yet realized that the message of light bulbs was information.[5]

From today's perspective, the concept that General Electric is, in fact, in the information-moving business has been fully realized under the direction of recently retired Chairman and CEO, Jack Welch. There are many current examples of companies that understand the nature of their business as Medium, and those that seemingly do not.

The Business Medium "Let Me See Your Palm"

Palm, Inc. realized that it has two distinct businesses, hardware and software. Each of these has different Messages, that is, the changes effected by each business. One could consider the effects of a portable hardware device with a touch screen, expandable via add-on modules, an infrared link capability and synchronization via an active computer link. On the other hand, one could consider the distinct effects of an extensible, relatively open operating environment designed for limited memory, display and peripheral-capability devices. Each, as has been demonstrated by the market, has considerable viability and unique cachet among various target customers.

Recognizing this, Palm licensed its software to other companies that would be potential competitors to its hardware business. Then, in January 2002, Palm created PalmSource Inc., a wholly owned subsidiary, so that two distinct companies could independently focus on hardware and software, respectively. In doing so, Palm's possible strategy recalls the hardware/software separation that contributed to the market dominance of the "WinTel" alliance — Intel's computer architecture representing hardware, Microsoft Windows, software.

This becomes particularly interesting when we compare the Palm's success with the unfortunate failure of an earlier personal digital assistant device, the Apple Newton. When the Newton was first introduced, much was made of the cool, new device. This was in keeping with Apple's self-image as a cool, hip computer company. Unfortunately, because there was little focus on how the Newton could change its users in the sense of "we shape our tools and thereafter our tools shape us," the Newton failed.

Interestingly, it may be that this lesson is not yet appreciated by Apple's management, who now seem to rely on cosmetics to spur growth, through changing the shape and colours of its iMac and iPod products. One could argue that it is the current penetration and incumbency of Windows-based software throughout the business world that has restricted Apple's business-oriented growth. The notable exception to this is in the graphics-related market where it has enjoyed past successes and market- / mind-share, precisely because the McLuhanesque Message of that market was well understood, although, it seems, entirely by accident. That management was unaware of its actions relative to a McLuhanesque *ground* is unfortunate. Apple's limitation in the general business market may well be the outcome of Apple's management legacy: The hip visionaries ironically ignored the McLuhanesque "multi-Media" nature of their business, refused to license MacOS to potential hardware competitors except for a brief, half-hearted period and were unsuccessful in developing parallel businesses.[6]

What is significant in considering the example of Apple is the understanding that the product — Macintosh and its descendants — represents two distinct, but obviously connected and related Media: The hardware platform and the software environment. This is consistent with McLuhan's contention that each Medium contains others — at least one and possibly more. From the perspective of commercial offerings, each component Medium can be a distinct offering, and the amalgam can itself be an offering — yet another Medium.

This concept of one Medium containing others, and how they are manifested will be explored later in greater depth. For now, think of a Medium having the potential to bring with it the effects of other things. Metaphorically, this may suggest stacking Russian dolls to some; others may envision the Trojan Horse. To some extent, both are correct.

Do the above examples of Palm and Apple suggest that a company that is "multi-Media" should always spin off its components into independent businesses? Not necessarily. Each path is accompanied by its own sets of effects, both direct and indirect, that must be carefully contemplated.

McLuhanistic Media Acceleration

Businesses, particularly technology businesses, fall in love with their innovations and gadgetry. However, this love affair is not limited to the TNT sector. At various times, the financial industry became enamoured with its own derivative wizardry, healthcare reveres new equipment and designer medications, airlines covet bigger and faster aircraft, and energy companies worship all of the above! We lust after the latest technological gadgetry and collectively gush, "Isn't this cool?" We then wonder how the business responsible for the coolness could fail.

The early 2000s witnessed the massive collapse of businesses that were entirely based on what could be accomplished technologically, in other words, the content of their Medium. There was little concern or understanding for what the collective effects of that technology might

Poets and artists live on frontiers. They have no feedback, only feedforward ... They are probes. Culture is Our Business, 1970

be — the Message of the Medium. To this day, most business analysts still miss the point of the TNT implosion. To be sure, we all understand the "how" of the collapse: Little or no revenue combined with a high burn rate simply resulted in the fledgling enterprises running out of cash. Combine this with the fact that these pseudo-businesses were financed on completely unrealistic valuations, and the rest is literally history by now. However, most business leaders, analysts and pundits still don't appreciate the "why."

A simple reduction of the McLuhan Equation is captured in the old adage of the so-called solution salesman, "People don't buy technology, they buy what technology will do for them."[7] The relationship between a new technology or Medium and "what it will do for them" is analogous to our earlier understanding of the relationship between *figure* and *ground*. In very simple terms, the *ground* provides the context. It is the *figure's* relationship with the *ground* that gives meaning to the *figure*. New *ground* means new meaning in each case, even for a constant *figure*.

Extending this notion, the Message — that is, the changes effected by the Medium — gives meaning to the Medium. So to answer the "what will it do for them" question about a product or service offering, for example, one must consider its real meaning. What changes in scale, pace or pattern does it effect? What are the consequences? How will feedforward change us — the people and companies that created the offering?

Every time the Message changes, that is, every time we are affected differently by a Medium, there is a new meaning, even for a constant Medium. The feedforward effects, which in the case of TNT companies happened at "Internet speed," changed the meaning of these companies' Media — their products, services, business models. And, in the context of these kaleidoscopic Media dynamics and a network of simultaneous effects enabled by the Internet that McLuhan termed "all-at-onceness," companies were incapable of keeping up. Thousands of companies and millions of people experienced McLuhanistic Media Acceleration at light speed.

Exhilarating, wasn't it?

Acceleration is a formula for dissolution and breakdown in any organization.

Understanding Media, 1966

In a practical sense, no one can truly imagine or predict all the consequential iterations of such acceleration. Why? Because we are limited by our *ground* — our current culture, business, society and environment. Our predictions are limited by our abilities to perceive what is actually happening and to invest these happenings with meaning. As we have seen, once the *ground* changes, so too does the meaning. Without the ability to perceive the present as it actually is, we cannot understand the Messages of our Media. We need to be able to understand today, before thinking about tomorrow.

Living in the Rear-View Mirror

Unfortunately it is supremely difficult to understand tomorrow's likely events. In fact, McLuhan tells us that most of us are not aware of what is happening today! He noted that, with very few exceptions, we are all facing backward, all keen observers of what came before, backing into the future.

Think of new products and technologies. The first use of any new technology is to replicate the capabilities of the old technology that it displaces. For example, telegraph replicated the news-carrying ability of newspapers and railways. Later, radio — "Marconi's Wireless" — replicated the telegraph before developing an identity of its own for delivering entertainment, sports and weather. Television was "radio with pictures," until its unique characteristics were understood and extended by entertainers such as Milton Berle and Sid Caesar (comedy/variety shows), Jackie Gleason (situation comedy) Jack Paar (the talk show) and events like the Kennedy/Nixon debate (political manipulation and "spin-doctoring").

Now, the Internet is viewed by some as "personal television," delivered on-demand to everyone's desktop. The Internet is a particularly interesting case, as its potential backward-looking uses are many. In addition to becoming a television surrogate, it was, among other things, cast as suburban shopping mall, mail-order catalogue and non-stop advertising channel. As we begin to understand the nature of the Internet and its various characteristics, our use of it will evolve.

The following admittedly abridged history of database software follows a similar pattern. The first computer "databases" were stacks of punch cards that repeatedly sorted and resorted, according to certain selection criteria. The advent of new technological capabilities — magnetic storage devices and core memory — saw the creation of electronic files, which were first sorted and resorted, as were their cardboard-based predecessors. Later, new ways of managing these so-called flat files were developed as their unique characteristics were realized. Hierarchical databases were then invented and were dutifully used to emulate flat files. Relational databases, now exceedingly powerful for commercial data management and queries, were first used to simply rebuild and re-implement hierarchical databases. Finally, when object-oriented techniques were first developed, their initial usage was based on the relational metaphor.

In every case, the new future-looking Medium is first used to rebuild the present. The same holds true for other Media as well. As we attempt to control their usage, to a great extent we place a governor on the Media's Messages. Because we cannot comprehend the changes in scale, pace and pattern, we attempt first to deny them, then to control them — often to our disadvantage. Observing that we almost universally turn our backs on the future, McLuhan called this "living in the rear-view mirror." In an interview, he noted:

> People live in the rear-view mirror because it's safer, they've been there before, they feel comfort. … The present is an area that people have always avoided throughout history – the utopias of mankind are all rear-view images of the preceding age… to live right on the shooting line, right on the frontier of change is terrifying.[8]

The Probing Mind

Imagine how successful a manager might be if he or she had the courage to truly live — and manage — in the present, "right on the frontier of change," with complete awareness. Of course, along with the courage comes the challenge of dealing with the all-at-onceness phenomenon: Being able to make some sense of the myriad simultaneous effects of many interacting Media and changing grounds. Even a manager well experienced in McLuhan's world, able to look beyond content and information in favour of effects, risks Media/Message over-

> **It may be said that the most valuable personal skill for an effective manager is ignorance.**

load. This is what we experienced, with McLuhanistic acceleration, through our initial infatuation with the Internet.

In a world of instantaneous communications and all-at-onceness, the most precious and valuable commodity to be sought is attention. Think about it: Every advertiser, every potential vendor and company desperately wants your attention, and will go to great, and sometimes outrageous, lengths to obtain it. Hence, it may be said that the most valuable personal skill for an effective manager is ignorance, literally *ignore-ance* — the ability to selectively and appropriately ignore irrelevant *figures* scattered amongst the *ground*. In this context, ignorance is not bliss — it is the practical manifestation of acute awareness and heightened perception.

Now, please go back and reread the previous paragraph, if you haven't already done so. Consider what we have just advocated: Ignorance as a valuable management skill. If you are like most people, some alarm bells of incredulity have just gone off in the back of your mind. Congratulations. You have just experienced the first, and most important, McLuhanesque thinking tool — the probe.

Probes were sent into space to investigate the unknown reaches of our solar system by sending back remote telemetry. Similarly, McLuhan used thinking probes to investigate unknown situations, new Media and changing circumstances. Like its physical counterpart, a probe prods our minds into action, forcing us to stop and think, because its effect on our consciousness is so unexpected. As an investigative tool, a probe is invaluable because it does not necessitate defending a conclusion or pre-conceived notion, nor does it require rigorous, scientific proof. It can be used to test serious, sardonic or simply silly hypotheses, not for their accuracy or adherence to a particular model of reality, but for their inherent probative or exploratory value. One good probe deserves another... and another... and another, until a fuller understanding, insight and awareness of Media and their Messages can be achieved. But McLuhanesque probing is more than simple questioning. As he reminds us, to achieve awareness, "one must probe everything ... including the words ... and oneself."[9]

Marshall McLuhan made a career out of probing. His writings are the journals of those investigative journeys and provide something of a roadmap to the workings of his mind. Or, perhaps a *treasure* map is a better metaphor, for the probing techniques we will explore later in the book will help today's managers and executives find the El Dorado of business management.

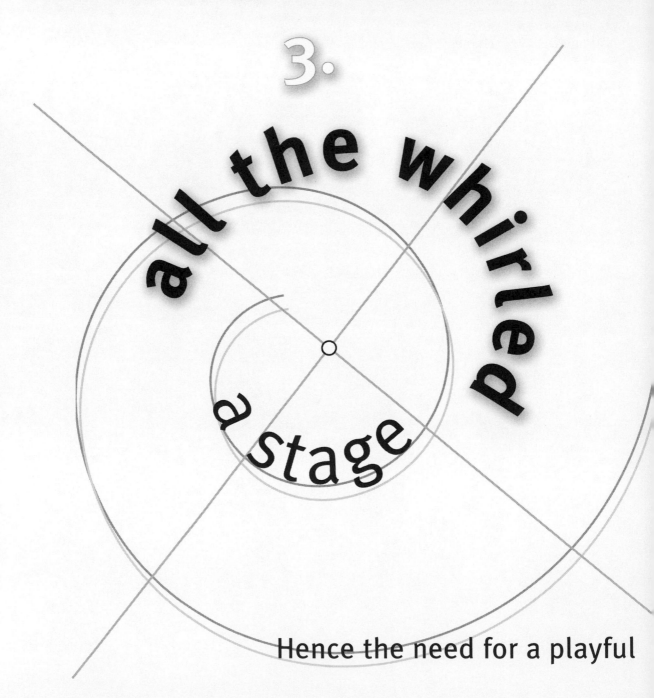

"Clear out the experts...The expert doesn't know

3.

all the whirled

a stage

Hence the need for a playful

the right questions, so he rejects the right answer.

and spontaneous approach to real problems."

—Take Today: The Executive as Dropout, 1972

Soon after learning to notice what you haven't noticed lately, it may be appropriate to wonder why you haven't noticed it lately. This recognition of awareness is especially important with respect to a business environment in which you are immersed nearly every day. In the rear-view mirror, clarity of vision and surety of decision making is perfect. It is easy for anyone to pick yesterday's stock market winners or play armchair CEO. Of course, when faced with trouble, it is seductively tempting to blame the scapegoat of the day — a financial crisis in Asia, deregulation of a market, expansion of free trade zones, globalization effects or the collapse of technology stocks. At times, the chorus of echoed explanations from disappointed chief executives would be humorous if not for the unfortunate fact that a one-size-fits-all excuse usually fits no one well.

It is particularly sad to watch a beleaguered corporate leader embrace the common scapegoat when other reasons are clearly evident. When casual observers can easily identify intrinsic shortcomings in business strategy or the inability of a management team to properly implement the operating plan, it is time for the executive to realize that he or she may be surprisingly unaware of the company's reality — a reality that must eventually be faced.

It is too easy to claim that executives or senior managers in such a predicament are merely in a state of denial. It is equally simplistic to blame their apparent unwillingness to accept reality on the executive's ego or blind ambition, although there are a cadre of corporate leaders to whom this may apply.

Scapegoat or not, the senior management team knows something is rotten in the state of the company — of this there is no doubt. External forces are apparently to blame, but shareholders demand recompense. Managers throughout the company spring into action, cutting jobs, reducing sundry expenses, shuttering plants and cutting back production. New systems initiatives are announced to better manage the supply chain and customer relationships. Strategy task forces are struck, bringing together the brightest lights of the global enterprise into a corporate brain trust. Consultants, both fresh-faced and grey-haired, swarm the corridors with market studies and facilitated strategy sessions involving hand-picked subject matter experts. Much frenzied activity ensues.

At the next annual meeting, the Chief Executive is either lauded as a visionary hero for engineering a tremendous turnaround, or rebuked as "the goat," echoing the comic strip character, Charlie Brown's self-deprecating description. There is rarely middle ground. However, the more inquisitive among us — shareholders, customers, suppliers or merely observers and pundits — are left to wonder why the actions of Executive Hero are to be praised, while those of Executive Goat are to be shunned, given that both essentially did the same thing. Granted, the outcomes were different — diametrically opposite, in fact. Nonetheless, it is widely assumed that the decisive actions of the hero were responsible for the improvement, but the goat's mismanagement should be punished with an early retirement followed by cover story castigation in the business magazines. But both did essentially the same thing.

Unfortunately, no one notices that in all likelihood, both executives' attention and awareness were primarily focused on the symptoms of their respective company's problems. The true nature and root causes of the problems may well have been hidden. As a result, the executives may equally have had little awareness of whether the actions which were to be taken would appropriately address the intrinsic issues. As has happened many times before, the executives, moved to action in good faith, might have jumped to solution, based on some combination of industry best practices, tried-and-true business school case study recipes and perhaps even study notes from "Frequent Flyer University."

Enter the Language Police

There are certain tell-tale clues that often indicate expedient fixes born of incomplete awareness: Quick and fresh management practices are often heralded by a new vocabulary, invented by their respective gurus or proponents. The new jargon often assumes a life of its own and the original intention of the practice, no matter how valid or initially useful, becomes diluted. Although the new language is frequently imprecise — unfortunately, often deliberately so — its further dilution by freshly indoctrinated practitioners results in the language deteriorating into little more than affectation.

The new buzzwords quickly become the object of ridicule and derision by the staff. Almost every employee in a large corporation today is familiar with the subversive pastime commonly known as "Buzzword Bingo" (or less politely, "BS Bingo"). This game is played to the chagrin of meeting organizers and the delight of bored, non-productive attendees. During a jargon-laden meeting, each participant uses a grid laid out like a conventional Bingo card. Instead of numbers, each square of the grid contains a buzzword or overused euphemism of faddish management practice. As the meeting progresses, the first mention of a word in a player's grid results in it being crossed off. When the entire grid is complete, the winning player shouts out, "Bullsh…" or something equally appropriate. In some companies, a winner is declared within minutes of beginning the meeting.

Many of these buzzwords have emerged from the management-consulting lexicon, often intoned with almost pontifical reverence by young consultants, new MBA graduates with the ink freshly dry on their diplomas. At one time, most of these terms had a meaning that was well understood, at least by their inventor. Now, however, the understanding has been lost as the meaning morphs to suit the speaker—a latter day *Through the Looking-Glass* in which "words mean precisely what I want them to mean."[1]

This is by no means a new phenomenon. Throughout modern history, language has been abducted by those who would use it to advance their own objectives with little resistance from the people adversely affected. As a chilling example, Marshall McLuhan directs us to George Orwell's *1984*. This novel, set in Orwell's future from the perspective of 1948, describes a dystopian society in which "thoughtcrimes" were severely punished. Acceptable language in the society was called "Newspeak." In the story, one of the society's linguists, Syme, describes its chilling purpose:

> Don't you see that the whole aim of Newspeak is to narrow the range of thought? In the end we shall make thoughtcrime literally impossible, because there will be no words in which to express it. Every concept that can ever be needed will be expressed by exactly one word, with its meaning rigidly defined and all its subsidiary meanings rubbed out and forgotten. Every year, fewer and fewer words, and the range of consciousness always a little smaller…[2]

While not exactly indicative of a dystopian society, modern management practice nonetheless seeks to "reinvent" language with the objective of limiting thinking to a preconceived and often hidden agenda.

Re-Engineering Business Process Re-Engineering

In the mid-1990s, the concept of Business Process Re-engineering (BPR) was promoted by Michael Hammer and James Champy in their popular work, *Re-engineering the Corporation: A Manifesto for Business Revolution*. In it, they describe a method of redesigning the processes within a company by which it is run and managed. The authors advocated beginning with a "blank sheet" in order to redesign the operations of the company from scratch, thereby increasing efficiency and effectiveness, resulting in potentially significant cost savings.

Although not necessarily intended by Hammer and Champy, BPR was the justification by which senior management initiated massive rounds of layoffs under the banner of "downsizing." This word — much like Orwell's Newspeak — was an attempt to euphemistically blunt the psychological effects of mass firings on unprotected employees who had become, courtesy of Hammer and Champy's *Manifesto*, disposable assets of the corporation. The term "downsizing," together with the BPR phrase itself, quickly fell into disrepute as cynical survivors of downsizing purges quickly translated the new jargon. In response, clever managers and consultants modified the jargon and invented the word, "rightsizing," which was considered more politically sensitive to those who had not yet been laid off.

This subtle but important tweak to management's verbal arsenal was meant to convey that subsequent layoffs were somehow "right" — the "right" decision for the company's future, creating an organization of the "right" size for success. The effect of language is so powerful that the word "rightsizing" even imbued a sense of being morally "right," much to the chagrin of the unfortunate numbers freshly awaiting unemployment cheques. However, modifying the language seemed to work: Decibel level of protests decreased. The use of the new euphemism apparently had a somewhat anesthetic effect.

The "right" word is not the one that names the thing but the word that gives the effect of the thing. Take Today: The Executive as Dropout, 1972

Language As Medium

As one might expect, language and speech held special significance for Marshall McLuhan. Our phonetic alphabet, with each letter-symbol representing a sound without any meaning of its own, is a human invention. The alphabet and the languages it builds are tools for organizing and structuring thoughts in our minds. McLuhan observed that language acts as metaphor: It transforms a set of abstract symbols — letters grouped into words — into mental images. The inside of our head becomes a kind of theatre in which our thoughts are the actors, performing roles scripted by language.

In the sense that humans created language, it is a technology or tool.

In the sense that humans created language, it is a technology or tool. As a Medium, language extends our thoughts from within our minds, making them available to others outside of us. McLuhan tells us that speech contains "an actual process of thought, which is in itself nonverbal."[3] McLuhan writes extensively about how language enabled the "tribal society," and how the later technology of electricity extends language-mediated consciousness to the now-ubiquitous "Global Village."[4]

We created language. In fact, we continue to create language, shaping this powerful tool as needed. Sometimes the need is born from self-preservation in the face of difficult circumstances. As we have just seen in the example of BPR, our need is frequently one of expediency in implementing management objectives. For example, reshaping language may be the only way to convert poor fiscal results to a form somewhat acceptable to shareholders. If earnings, circa 1980, are unacceptable and significantly below expectations, reshape the word "earnings" into EBITDA — earnings before interest, taxes, depreciation and amortization. Voilà! 1980s-style losses are now 2000s-style operating or "pro forma" earnings, before accounting for one-time, special, exceptional, non-cash charges and restatement of results from prior quarters, as described in the auditor's footnotes.

In the sense of McLuhan's view that "we shape our tools and thereafter our tools shape us,"[5] language has proven to be a particularly potent Medium for shaping us. Language influences our behaviour and directs our perception of reality. His fascination with language focused on, among other things, its intimate link with human thought.

To Tell the Truth

According to McLuhan, we discern reality by matching an external observation to an internal set of patterns — a model of sorts — that represents our conception of the nature of the universe, or at least our small corner thereof. When there is a successful match between what we perceive and what we conceive — between outer and inner — we believe we have found Truth. When we cannot match our outer perception to our inner conception of reality, we literally do not believe our eyes or ears — whatever we sense "cannot be true."[6]

Language influences our behaviour and directs our perception of reality.

This realization makes Truth less of an absolute and more of a relative condition. It also gives us valuable clues on how relative Truth is managed in the business environment. There are two available mechanisms. The first one can alter our ability to make valid external observations, say by dulling perception. Euphemisms and invented, positive-sounding words hung onto negative actions serve this purpose. Allowing ourselves to ignore what is wrong, or establishing a business climate in which "bad news" is discouraged also dulls perception. The second one can reshape our internal model by using the Message — the thought-altering effects of the Medium, language.

In fact, language is such a powerful Medium, that it can accomplish both actions simultaneously. Language can hold consciousness captive and thereby render objective observation impossible. Our perception of relative Truth can be managed and manipulated as described by the McLuhan Equation. "The Medium is the Message" in this case tells us that language has the power to directly influence our perception, thoughts and action. While this power is often deployed for expedient self-interest, we will later see how it can also be used as a probe — a powerfully constructive and positive thinking tool.

Hitachi Data Systems (HDS)

In the late 1980s, Hitachi Data Systems was preparing to make a significant assault on IBM's dominance in the mainframe computer and peripherals market. At the time, HDS was the number three supplier of IBM-compatible equipment for the data centre, lagging far behind its arch-rival Amdahl Corporation in actual sales and market — that is, customer — perception. This market position existed despite having, by many accounts, technologically superior equipment offered at lower prices. As one part of the "makeover" process, a newly appointed sales and marketing executive engaged a small team of consultants. Their objective was to change internal attitudes and behaviours through mandatory employee leadership training. Of primary importance was modification of the language used by all employees, especially when referring to themselves in the context of peers, superiors and subordinates.

> **If we look at new language or jargon as a Medium, what is its Message?**

Terms like "manager," "employee" and "co-worker" were abolished and banned from all internal communication. There were no superiors or subordinates, nor direct or indirect reports. Instead, the entire population of the American-run subsidiary of this Japanese multi-national company ironically referred to one another as "colleagues" in a manner distinctly reminiscent of the Cold War Russian appellation, "comrade." All colleagues were equal, but some colleagues, with an acknowledgment to Orwell's *Animal Farm*, "were more equal than others."[7] These were the leaders who, not so surprisingly, held positions rather similar to the managers and executives of the previous regime.

Because everyone was an equal colleague, everyone was therefore an equal participant in the unified struggle against the number one and number two competitors. However, everyone was expected to make sacrifices for the common good and follow the regimen dictated by those responsible for central planning, processes and procedures. Among other things, there were onerous requirements for specifically prescribed reporting at all levels and significantly reduced autonomy for local leadership.

In this extreme example, language was severely compromised in an attempt to modify and control behaviour. It worked, but only for a short time — the ultimate result was a revolution of sorts, and the relegation of the word "colleague" to the linguistic recycle bin. To this day, many survivors of that period at HDS cringe at the use of the word colleague, especially if it is used to address the person to whom one is speaking.[8]

By now, twisting language in an attempt to control and influence thinking is well understood and has advanced to a high art form throughout business and politics. There are those who have made a career of it, known in some contexts as "spin doctors," and in others as management consultants. In either case, new language is created, but not necessarily to convey radically new ideas that cannot be expressed in any other way. Throughout history, new ideas have been quite adequately communicated using pre-existing words to which everyone can relate. It is only on the rare historical occasion, when truly revolutionary or innovative discoveries have been made, that new words are required. In such cases, current language is insufficient to capture the new concepts.

In most instances of management practice, however, new language is regularly created in order to begin the process of modifying and controlling internal perception. If we look at new language or jargon as a Medium, what is its Message? The effect of newly created jargon is at least two-fold. First, our thinking changes according to the frames of reference intended by the jargon's creators. Second, we change our perception of the scale or significance of the new, important ideas expressed by the jargon. We do not usually stop to consider whether the supposedly new or important ideas are indeed original, significant, noteworthy or even useful. Instead, we simply match our external perception of new jargon with our internal conception that new language equals a new or important idea, and we believe that we have been given a new, albeit relative, truth.

Management Clichés

Because new language connotes significance, managers are generally eager to embrace its promise of new and radical ideas. Given a chance, we could each recite a dozen examples of such new language off the top of our heads. Each held some promise of managerial salvation:

When "truth" is reduced to mere matching of inner and outer any statement can be questioned. From Cliché to Archetype, 1970

Total Quality Management, Knowledge Management, e-Commerce, B2B, B2C, New Economy, Enterprise Resource Planning, Customer Relationship Management, Convergence … Originally, each of these terms conveyed a concept that had some relative value. Originally, each of these terms had a meaning that was well understood by its creator and its early advocates. However, as jargon spreads throughout the business world, self-proclaimed experts appropriate the new terms and, in doing so, dilute and distort their meaning. Over time, these words become nothing more than management clichés — accepted by all, repeated by many, understood by almost none.

In fact, the concept of a management cliché extends beyond mere words: It includes oft-repeated management practices, behaviours, tactics, responses, decisions, strategies and plans that have long lost their context or meaning, and are often inappropriately applied. Recall the executive who sprung into action in response to fiscal results that came in short of expectations. His actions — laying off staff, slashing expense budgets, implementing new systems, hiring consultants and corralling the best and the brightest from among the ranks —are all too common. These have become instinctive, almost knee-jerk reactions to complex business challenges. To be sure, they are so common as to be considered management clichés themselves.

> **Management clichés are not only responses to dire circumstances. They are also common day-to-day occurrences in a mundane, work-a-day corporate office.**

Management clichés are not only responses to dire circumstances. They are also common day-to-day occurrences in a mundane, workaday corporate office. Think of the obligatory Status Meeting Without Agenda. Or the exercise of developing and posting the Corporate Mission Statement for all to see — and often ignore. And how about the ubiquitous PowerPoint Presentation, a cliché which one senior consultant has taken to calling "the *de facto* language of management."[9] In one instance, for example, a start-up company seeking to establish some sort of strategic alliance — another management cliché — with a household-name corporation in the TNT sector introduced itself via a PowerPoint Presentation. The presentation slides literally contained no substantive content that described the start-up's product or service offering, nor any terms of a proposed business arrangement. The company's principals clearly believed in the sufficiency of the PowerPoint

Medium itself. Their conception was that the Medium supplanted both the Message and the content.

As managers, we willingly adopt these cliché practices because they are convenient, widely accepted and frequently expected. They offer the path of least resistance to gaining approval for plans, since management clichés are rarely questioned by those in authority. "No one was ever fired for buying IBM," was the cautionary watch-phrase during the heyday of Big Blue. But more than assured acceptance and approval, management clichés provide a means for us to accomplish the tasks of the day without having to resort to the time- and effort-consuming process of engaging in original thought.

Internalizing Clichés

Marshall McLuhan provides some understanding of why management clichés are so readily accepted in the business world.[10] Throughout our busy lives — publicly, privately, corporately, individually — the unquestioned mass acceptance and adoption of clichés has had two profound and insidious effects. First, we internalize clichés as part of our psychological and intellectual lexicon. For example, during the summer of 2000, how many times did you hear (or utter!) the threat to "kick someone off the island," emulating the popular television show, *Survivor*? In 2001, a person not working up to his or her potential was told, "You *are* the Weakest Link. Goodbye."

By mimicking these tag lines in a business context we abdicate to television scriptwriters the task of communicating and explaining our thoughts and ideas, counting on pop culture to supply codified shorthand for both language and thought. Unfortunately, in doing so, we also abdicate the tasks of thinking, reasoning and making appropriate judgements by patterning our minds to favour quick, supposedly witty, one-liners. Similarly, by embracing management clichés as easy, ready-made solutions to difficult problems, managers abdicate their responsibility for making carefully considered decisions. The temptation to jump to a pre-fabricated solution is compelling.

The results of living inside a proscenium arch of satellites is that the young now accept the public spaces of the earth as role-playing areas.

From Cliché to Archetype, 1970

You Are Getting Sleepy...

McLuhan emphasizes that the second, and perhaps more dangerous, effect of clichés is to anaesthetize us. That is, clichés cause our awareness to shut off, leaving us in something of a trance-like state when it comes to calling on reasoning or thinking abilities. When cast against a business *ground*, we become oblivious to the effects of cliché practices and the beliefs that management clichés cause. This, in turn, has the overworked manager sleepwalking through significant management problems and issues, without realizing that his experience is little more than going through preconditioned motions. The price of this automatic response is high: It results in inappropriate decisions, repetition of prior mistakes — both one's own and those of others — complacency with the status quo, substitution of activity for action, and the almost-guaranteed inability to achieve sustainable success.

McLuhan focuses on the anesthetic effect of clichés on our consciousness and awareness. Anesthesia is the numbing of all the senses that results in a loss of awareness and the inability to perceive or appropriately respond to the environment. However, in the case of management practice, the anesthetic effect is not like that of surgery in which there is no consciousness whatsoever and the patient benefits from the absence of perception. It is more akin to catatonia or hypnosis: The subject is unaware of the surroundings, but nonetheless, highly suggestible. For example, we see untenable business practices, but don't observe their effects on cash flow until working capital has nearly been exhausted. We hear dissatisfied customers but cannot listen to their guidance or understand their perspective, especially if it requires our procedures to change. Managers may be touched, but cannot feel, as witnessed in the earlier example of BPR-justified downsizing.

During the height of the downsizing fad, managers had become anesthetized to the effects of mass firings and layoffs mandated by the management cliché of BPR. Consequently, they went far beyond cutting the "fat" that resulted from over-hiring during the good years. In continuing to cut into the corporate muscle and supporting skeletal structure, they could not feel the direct pain of company amputations in which

To the blind all things are unexpected.

Understanding Media, 1964

enterprises lost decades of aggregate experience and the accumulated proprietary knowledge of valuable employees. It is interesting to note the reaction that the BPR management cliché caused when it was extended beyond anything that could be considered reasonable. The resulting loss of the collective experience and know-how directly led to the mirror-image management cliché known as Knowledge Management.

BPR and the resulting loss of collective experience directly led to the mirror-image cliché known as Knowledge Management.

Management clichés serve to manage relative business truth through the dual, complementary mechanisms that we identified earlier — altering internal conception and dulling external perception. By creating a new language through the use of pervasive buzzwords, clichés compromise critical thinking, thereby creating a distorted internal conception of reality. By numbing perception, the anesthetic effect of management clichés prevents objective awareness by "demobilizing consciousness," as McLuhan puts it.[11]

Best Practices

Matching a new language to dulled observation reinforces slogans and self-serving principles, regardless of their lack of objective sense or intrinsic merit. By suppressing critical thinking, management clichés lull managers and executives into a sense of complacency and acceptance, with often serious consequences for their business, their employees and their own careers. Valuable time and resources are expended on management clichés with little to show for the time invested in actual sustainable results.

The extension of this, unfortunately, is worse than the wasted resources, and potentially more damaging. The managers of one company, with awareness and perception suitably dulled, will often adopt the processes and procedures of another company with little in the way of prior diligence. This predilection for rushing to deploy "best practices" is perhaps one of the more potentially dangerous management clichés of recent years.

A corporation faced with complex problems and market challenges seeks to remedy those problems quickly, so as not to fall further behind its peers. It looks at other companies in the same industry or field of endeavour and attempts to determine which of their management processes significantly contribute to their apparent success. Once identified, these processes, or rather, an abstraction of these processes, is adopted in the hope that their magical effect will attract analogous success to the challenged company.

Of course, there is no magic — no practice can be best for every company in any arbitrary situation. So how does the trick work? Successful companies, which those in trouble seek to emulate, generally possess the attribute of shared, insightful, original thinking among their managers and executives, and often through the ranks of their key employees. They identify challenges and carefully contemplate the particular circumstances and environment before determining a course of action. Often, the first solution is not successful and the process repeats. Eventually, a way out of the mire is discovered and the company progresses.

The resulting success attains almost mythic proportions, especially if the company is sufficiently prominent. In the retelling, the story is abridged and perhaps embellished for dramatic effect in a case study presented at a conference or in an article in the business press. It then enters the management concordance as an industry best practice.

However, for another company enamoured with the management cliché that is the condensed version of the story, the details are lost. The company's particular context and circumstances — the *ground* — are different from those of the original experience. The implementation in the original company's case was not a one-shot, packaged cure-all, but an evolving process, during which staff learned through several, progressively more successful, iterations. Even if the starting points of the two companies were similar, the Message of each iteration — the cumulative effects on the pioneering company — meant that the *ground* had significantly changed by the time the eventual solution was finally implemented.

Information channels become management clichés — a mass suppression of critical thinking leading to blind acceptance of their content.

Widening the Credibility Gap

Information channels themselves become management clichés. As their anesthetic effects become more pervasive, the result is a mass suppression of critical thinking and objective testing against reality, leading to blind acceptance of their content. For example, at one time, data presented by way of a printed, computer-generated report was considered gospel because everyone knew that computers did not make mistakes. For many years, television — particularly television news — was considered authoritative, with news anchors like Edward R. Murrow, Walter Cronkite, Chet Huntley and David Brinkley regarded among the most trustworthy people in America.

Today, the World Wide Web "demobilizes consciousness" by virtue of its users' clichéd acceptance of the Web as a convenient authoritative information source. The net effect of this clichéd stupor would be humorous, if it was not so terribly frightening in its implications. Consider these relatively recent examples that would likely not have occurred but for the anesthetic effect of the Web as cliché:

- According to Pierre Salinger, former press secretary in the Kennedy administration, among others, TWA flight 800 that crashed off the coast of Nantucket Island in July 1996 was brought down by an errant U.S. Navy missile.

- Jonathon Lebed, among many, many others, allegedly perpetrated extensive stock price manipulation through posting multiple misleading messages on Web-based message boards. Among many interesting aspects of this particular case is the fact that Jonathon Lebed was 15 years old at the time.

- Marcus Arnold, another 15-year-old posing as a lawyer, dispensed legal advice to many people via the relatively anonymous AskMe.com. Despite his only legal "qualifications" being that he watched courtroom dramas on television and the Court TV cable network, he quickly became AskMe.com's highest-rated legal advisor. This case is particularly interesting from the perspective of the McLuhan Equation, as it comments profoundly on the cliché effects of the Web as well as television script writers and the legal profession itself.

Arguably, this sampling is merely illustrative of the Internet's ability to widely propagate information, regardless of its accuracy or the reliability of its source. We would not disagree: Were it not for the Internet's capability as an effective mode of information transport, these cases would not have occurred as they did. Other modes of information transport have been used for decades to perpetrate frauds and hoaxes upon an unsuspecting public. Everything from telephone "boiler room" stock fraud scams to Orson Wells's *War of the Worlds* radio hoax have relied on mass communications as the distribution vehicle. However, at some point between sensory perception and the consequent human action, the brain, of necessity, was involved. McLuhan notes that "Truth becomes Trust, not Cartesian certainty,"[12] when the mind's perception is dulled by the action of cliché. It is precisely this loss of rationality that the hoaxers and connivers count on.

In the business context, it is frightening to contemplate what might happen when such a loss of rationality combines with language's ability to gain control of one's conception. Considering language as a Medium, its Message is powerful indeed. However, such a consideration also reveals a clue as to how language can be used to combat perception control. More than that, language is also the key to gaining new, insightful perceptions about the business environment. In this sense, Buzzword Bingo, is more than a cynical diversion. It is the first line of defence.

> **Buzzword Bingo is more than a cynical diversion. It is the first line of defence.**

"The Boy Returned Home with a Cliché on His Face"[13]

With apologies to Shakespeare, consider these lines of verse:

> All the stage is a world,
> And all the players, merely men and women.
> They have their excitements and their trances.
> And one part, in its time, is played by many actors.
> It ages. A being in many acts.[14]

When we hear the original soliloquy — "All the world's a stage and all the men and women merely players," and so forth — our minds subconsciously say, "Oh yes, I know this one," as the words flow through our restful consciousness like a familiar tune. On the other hand, as we read the previous passage, our consciousness detects a dissonance — there is something somehow familiar, yet distinctly different about this twisted version of the character Jacques' frequently recited monologue. This involuntary realization causes our sensibility to sit up and pay attention; our psyche to perk up much like a hound that has just caught a scent of the prey. Just as a cliché will dull critical thinking, twisting the language of the cliché heightens awareness and primes the intellect.

McLuhan calls this process "sharpening the cliché into a probe."[15] Here is McLuhan probing the cliché itself :

> A teacher asked her class to use a familiar word in a new way. One boy read: "The boy returned home with a cliché on his face." Asked to explain his phrase, he said, "The dictionary defines cliché as a 'worn out expression.'"[16]

In the context of investigating business problems, management clichés are indeed "worn out expressions" — expressions of over-used business approaches that have worn out their usefulness. Over a relatively short period, most had been prescribed as a panacea but were inappropriately applied by managers and consultants who had forgotten — or perhaps never knew — the original context or meaning of these practices. However, when management clichés are sharpened into probes, they can be deployed as the entry point to an exploration of alternative approaches.

Buzzword Bingo takes the first step toward heightening our sensitivity to the proliferation of management clichés. Rather than allow the clichés to deaden our consciousness, the game first forces the participants to identify and react to any of the selected clichés being used. Even this minimal level of heightened awareness nullifies the stupefying effect of the cliché and draws attention to its relative lack of meaning. Those who are experienced players can subsequently scan and sift marketing bumf, job placement advertisements, mission and vision statements — clichés in their own right — and other sundry artifacts of corporate newspeak. An added benefit — regular players will either tend not to use such clichés themselves, or, if required, use them accompanied by a strong dose of irony.

Buzzword Bingo takes the first step toward heightening our sensitivity to the proliferation of management clichés.

Once such awareness is awakened, the next step is to gain new insight into the issue for which a management cliché has been the superficial answer. This is accomplished by using the Medium of language, and its Message for causing changes in thought. In sharpening the cliché into a probe, we quicken the

In sharpening the cliché into a probe, we quicken the pace of thinking and creatively alter patterns of thought.

pace of thinking and creatively alter patterns of thought. By doing so, the scale and scope of thought are expanded, with the aim of discovering a new approach to a problem, or retrieving a long-forgotten solution. Even if aspects of the management cliché are found to be truly applicable, managers can be assured that such a conclusion is the result of a mind freed from a long, often unwitting slumber.

From Management Cliché to Probe

There are many techniques for sharpening a cliché into a probe. Perhaps the simplest method is to use punning or word associations to change the management cliché phrase. For example, a product manager may seek to gain the "competitive edge" in her company's market. But if you look carefully at what is actually accomplished, the competitive edge may, in fact, be a *repetitive edge*. The product manager may want to look closely at marketing plans to determine whether contemplated actions are simply a matter of an old *whine* in a new bottle. Or, if the company believes it must play catch-up with the competition, some careful scenario planning may prevent the pursued competitive edge from becoming a competitive *cliff*.

Another example: Total Quality Management was a management cliché greatly touted by many consulting firms and adopted to some extent by companies throughout the world. In each context, TQM had its own particular twist, and many books were written on the subject by a variety of academics, consultants and proponents. Naturally, obligatory measurement and reporting systems were established with metrics galore. It seemed that Total Quality Management became Total *Quantity* Management with the assistance of outside consulting firms, each of whom was keenly interested in Total *Wallet-y* Management.

Reverend William Archibald Spooner, a British cleric and warden of New College at Oxford at the turn of the twentieth century, became famous for his "spoonerisms." These linguistic *faux pas* are characterized by interchanging the initial letters or sounds of two or more words to humorous effect. Taking some poetic licence, technology that is described as "state of the art" could determine the *fate of the start*, or for fans of the irreverent cartoon, *South Park*, the *state of the f…* You get the idea. Interchanging entire words for a new meaning is also fair game.

Two words that sound alike but have different meanings are called homophones, like "The *reign* in Spain…" Similarly, two words that are spelled alike, but have different meanings are homographs. Think of the old chestnut, "Time flies like an arrow; fruit flies like a banana." Both homophones and homographs make excellent cliché sharpeners. For example, in the 1980s, Information Technology departments were known as Management Information Systems. Unfortunately, MIS management often represented *mis*management.

After the Internet bubble burst, dot-com companies became eerily dot-*calm*. It now seems that the hyped-up knowledge economy has been shown to be a *no-ledge* e-conomy. However, had its proponents been confronted with this cliché probe before the crash, the implications of "no ledge" may have offset some of the unjustified exuberance and allowed time for appropriate business contingencies to be established.

Substituting a synonym for one of the words in a management cliché also may give rise to a new perspective. For example, companies will speak about their "value statement." However, substituting *invoice* for statement provides a whole new view of the issue: For a particular customer, what is the tally of the value *invoice*? Can sales and marketing managers specifically enumerate what the company has done to provide value and list it line by line? This sharpened cliché-probe may force new thinking about the company's relationship with its customers. Naturally, it is incumbent upon management not merely to provide a glib answer, but to probe deeply into all aspects of the issue that the probe has uncovered.

Specific vocalizations can be used to construct a cliché-probe. McLuhan refers to Edward T. Hall's book, *The Silent Language*, and its identification of the "superfix."[17] This term, coined analogously to prefix or suffix, refers to "going over or above the utterance" in order to convey meaning by one of voice, emphasis, degree of loudness or stress:

> For example, in English the difference in the spoken language between
> green house (the colour green), greenhouse (where plants are grown)

and the Green house (owned by Mr. and Mrs. Green) is solely a function of varying stress.[18]

Of course, one might say the same about managers' responses to challenges.

The Archetype: Cliché Retrieved

Finally, a new management cliché may force recollection of an old cliché that brings with it something that McLuhan called "retrieved awareness." This is a particularly interesting instance, since prior over-usage may have consigned the old cliché to the management scrap heap. However, in the face of a current management cliché, the intrinsic value of the older term may be recalled as an archetype. By using this mechanism, consciousness awakes as the flash of insight results in new understanding being instantly achieved in the present-day context.

Consciousness awakes as the flash of insight results in new understanding being instantly achieved in the present-day context.

One of the best examples of the evolution of a management cliché from a legitimate proposition, through a period of overuse and co-option, and finally to retrieval as an archetype is the term "Paradigm Shift." Although the term had existed for some time, it gained popularity and became firmly ensconced in management's lexicon as a result of a 1993 book by Don Tapscott and Art Caston, *Paradigm Shift: The New Promise of Information Technology.*[19] The book deals with the perceived change in the way information technology is used in organizations. The authors make the argument that a new model of computing is necessary to position corporations for business transformation in the future.

At the time, very few practising managers were familiar with the meaning of the word paradigm and fewer still could comprehend or accept the implications of its shift. Still, the word ricocheted off the walls of conference lecture halls like buckshot off a tin roof. Soon, consultants of every ilk were shifting paradigms, or warning of their impending relocation. Managers were planning for or worrying about whether their own paradigms — and budgetary *pair o' dimes* — were shifting. The term eventually lost its cachet and vanished from the business press prior to the rise of the Internet's popularity.

Time passed and so-called New Media became the *New Mania*. Imaginative models for businesses that were to work in "Internet time" were proposed, many of which had no grounding in even basic economics. We now know most of the new valuation metrics and business models were mere fantasies, figments of popular market analysts' and some venture capitalists' overactive and greedy imaginations. However, among some of the more prudent analysts and commentators, the management cliché of a "new business model" was sharpened into a probe by retrieving, as archetype, the question of whether or not the general business *paradigm* had truly shifted.

A Child's Work Is Play. An Adult's Play Is...

When using the technique of sharpening a management cliché into a cliché-probe, it is important to maintain a humorous and playful approach. When one is too deadly serious about these sorts of probing, the mind becomes far too analytical. There are sufficient analytical approaches to most business problems; conventional responses represent *ground* well covered. In seeking new insights and approaches to thinking about problems, we need to travel another path, one that is less analytical and serious, one more akin to play. Over-analysis restricts the mind's freedom and creativity, automatically editing, filtering and sorting all of the potentially irrational ideas. However, it is out of the irrational and chaotic that possible new approaches and fresh viewpoints can emerge. Perhaps the best enabler of irrationality is humour.

You may have chuckled while reading some of the examples cited previously. Indeed, in group cliché-probe sessions, the atmosphere often becomes downright rowdy — and sometimes randy as well. Creative energy flows through the minds of participants; the only ideas discarded out of hand are the *trite and true*. Frequently, session participants allow themselves to explore a more child-like state of mind as a path to unlocking creativity, discovery and learning.

Out of the irrational, new approaches can emerge. Perhaps the best enabler of irrationality is humour.

When it comes to one's ability to learn, children — particularly young children — have a tremendous capacity and a curious advantage over adults. In the first place, they have an incredible amount to learn — how to manage their bodies, how to speak, read, comprehend, how to understand the rules of the world — both physical and relational. They accumulate subject-specific knowledge and applied skills. All of this is largely accomplished within the first few years of life, and mostly completed, as far as it will be completed, within the first twenty to twenty-five years. After that, the adult's willingness to learn is often severely hindered, primarily by the individual's own attitude.

Children are not afraid to admit that they don't know something because there is no expectation that they should have *a priori* knowledge, at least up to a certain point of development. Further, until they observe and begin to mimic common adult behaviour, that is, that exploring and learning is somehow a negative reflection on the person's competence, they are keenly interested in acquiring knowledge with an almost insatiable curiosity. In homes in which there is a life-long love of learning, even by the adults, the children will not learn the lesson that exploring new ideas is atypical until, ironically, it is taught to them in school.

Adults often shun learning new things without a pressing motivation, responding with the ready excuse of "I'm too old to begin to learn that" or the saw about teaching old dogs new tricks. They certainly avoid venturing far from familiar and well-trodden mental pathways, particularly in an environment that rewards bureaucratic adherence to established procedures. In a management context, the convenient excuse is, "That's the way we've always done things around here." The key to being able to gain new insights and perceptions, that is, to be able to look at things in entirely new ways, is to become more childlike in our approach to thinking and developing mental relationships and connections. Hence, we should sharpen the management workshop cliché into the cliché-probe, *playshop*.

McLuhan actually emphasizes the importance of play and humour in the context of constructing cliché-probes. Referring to the tradition of the court jester, he writes:

> At another level, every emperor must have his clown... In rigid hierarchical societies only this licensed character dare exercise the probe of free speech. The clown is indispensable as audience-checker... Without his clown, the emperor has no means of contact with the public.[20]

We should sharpen the management workshop cliché into the cliché-probe, "playshop."

It is important to include the joker, the "class clown" and the cynic in the play of creating cliché-probes to tear down the mystique of management clichés and counter their deleterious effects. Jesters, clowns and skeptics have the right frame of mind with which to use cliché-probes to help regain awareness of business reality. Like the court jester of old, cliché-probes fulfill the vital role of challenging us to question often hidden, or not stated, assumptions. They help obtain new insights into problems in the face of pat, standard or pre-programmed responses.

Focus on Customer Focused

In one playshop, the participants had selected "customer focused" as one of the management clichés to be probed. In their organization, this was the latest watchword as the company sought to improve its relationship with its customers. Throughout the corporation, all new endeavours had to be shown to be "customer focused" in order for any initiative to be approved. Clearly, the participants were anxious to impale this term with a sharpened cliché-probe.

In the first round of the playshop, among other things, they came up with the following probes:

- Customer hocus-pocused
- Focused customer
- Customer magnified
- Customer concentrate (like frozen orange juice)

Some of these require a bit of explanation since they are presented here out of context. The first is clearly a word play, rhyming "focused" with *hocus-pocused*. This related to the perception by some that a sleight of hand or distraction was being perpetrated upon the customers in this latest corporate initiative. The third probe, *customer-magnified*, is a word association with "focused" being used in the sense of what would be accomplished with a magnifying glass. The last probe came from one participant thinking about the word "focus" as a synonym for *concentration*.

Survival ... will depend on the ability to probe ... in the proper way and place. As the ... environment is perpetually in flux, so the need is not for fixed concepts... Laws of Media: The New Science, 1988

This led the jokester in the group to jump from mental concentration to the verb concentrate, finally landing on the allusion to juice *concentrate*.

The next round of the playshop involves taking the sharpened cliché-probes on a journey through the participants' minds to explore possible ways in which the probe could shed new light on the issue at hand. In the discussion that ensued from *customer hocus-pocused*, there was serious concern expressed that customers may view the latest initiatives as little more than marketing and sloganeering. The company apparently had a history of accompanying analogous internal initiatives with considerable fanfare. Unfortunately, most resulted in little of lasting or tangible value as far as customers were concerned. The group's exploration tended toward contemplating mechanisms whereby nominally customer-focused initiatives could be required to demonstrate effects that would actually bring substantial benefits to customers.

The *focused customer* probe led to a rather lengthy discussion that examined the changing nature of the company's customers — clearly more focused on receiving value and more focused on the specific services that they could obtain from a variety of vendors as opposed to the previous notion of "one-stop shopping." This was a significant and remarkable insight for the group, as the company had always seen itself as a metaphorical department store in its market, attempting to be as many things to as many customers as possible. In doing so, and having made the strategic decision to continue in this vein, the company was terribly vulnerable. The group realized that their company was acting in opposition to the majority of its customers' current mode of buying. Further, since the company was organized and managed to be "all things to all people," its sales message was becoming confused, leaving it exposed to smaller, more nimble, and more focused competitors across many market segments.

The company was awash in market studies. However, there was little knowledge of how customers actually made buying decisions.

It was quickly becoming clear to the group that despite the executive's theme of becoming "customer focused," the company had very little actual understanding of its customers. This is not to say that it was not awash in market studies, segmentation analyses, market research reports, marketing plans and proposed advertising campaigns. However, there was little knowledge of how customers actually made their buying decisions and what were the key criteria that made the difference between a win and a loss.

This is where *customer magnified* and *customer concentrate* entered the discussion. These two probes became ways of exploring how actual customer decision making could be captured — concentrated — by appropriate sampling, and understood through insightful examination — magnifying. The group considered various mechanisms whereby true customer understanding could be injected into the company's ongoing processes. First, group managers noted that there was no consistent form of loss review when a major sales campaign was unsuccessful. Thus, any knowledge, experience and competitive information garnered from the campaigns were lost. Another participant probed the term "loss review" and asked the simple question, "What about a *win* review?" This probe led to the realization that no one quite knew how the company won business. Participants wondered if there were certain elements that were common to successful sales efforts. Certainly there was much more to specifically investigate with the sales department after the session.

Finally, by considering the probe, *customer concentrate*, several people embarked on a flight of fancy involving a vision of having such a concentrate — in powdered or frozen form — in the marketing department. "Just add water" and the customer would be reconstituted in order to test marketing initiatives. It was pointed out that the company regularly organized market research and focus groups. However, these occurred long after significant investments in new programs and products had been made. The customers tested in this way merely responded according to their preferences among limited choices, proposed in an artificial context.

After a brief tutorial on the McLuhanesque concepts of *figure* and *ground*, one person questioned whether the company could capture and understand the customer's *ground*. This question, when set against *customer concentrate* resulted in the realization that no one among the marketing staff had ever been a customer, using the company's products and services. They suggested to management that recruiting for the marketing department itself be "customer focused:" Where possible, new hires should be selected from among candidates who had been customers in the company's markets.

Through the structure of the playshop, the participants in this case took their current dominant management cliché, "customer focused," and literally played with it to produce an initial list of sharpened cliché-probes. From among the unfiltered and uninhibited initial list, certain probes were selected for serious, and sometimes not so serious, examination and discussion. Because their minds were freed from the restrictive weight of management's imperative, they were able to experiment with various ideas and concepts, delving into many issues that had never been discussed in any conventional context. After less than a day, which included "playshop training," several key recommendations were proposed and subsequently adopted. The term "customer focused" was also banished — at least for the time being.

The cliché-probe is an important tool for management. Managers' minds depart from the conventional and explore what might be considered somewhat irreverent or even irrational. Original thought and new approaches are allowed to break through. The cliché-probe awakens the modern manager from the somnambulism of management-by-assumption and management-by-fad. In fact, it may be the *best practice* a manager's awareness will get.

> "And hast thou slain the Jabberwock? Come to my arms, my beamish boy! O frabjous day! Callooh! Callay!" He chortled in his joy. "Jabberwocky," Lewis Carrol, *Through the Looking-Glass and What Alice Found There*

4. Introducing a New Crystal Ball

The Laws of Media

Tetrads

"Everybody experiences far more than he understands. Yet it is experience, rather than understanding that influences behavior, especially in collective matters of media and technology, where the individual is almost inevitably unaware of their effect upon him."

—Understanding Media, 1964

An immediate benefit of using McLuhan's awareness techniques — distinguishing *figure* from *ground*, and sharpening clichés into cliché-probes — is that insights appear at a remarkable pace. Our potential to discover possible new answers and alternatives to complex business issues greatly increases. This, however, is not entirely a good thing. A cornucopia of available alternatives would further burden modern managers, who already lament that they have insufficient time to properly think through all the ramifications of their decisions. Many harried managers respond with a quick fix, implementing a solution that is expedient and "good enough" for the moment.

This may seem to be an economical approach — find the answer, fix the problem and move on — but clearly, it may not be optimal. In the first place, the "good enough" answer may not, in fact, be the best approach. Second, a more thorough investigation may uncover other issues that are germane to the problem at hand. Third, quick implementations usually disregard effects that are not immediately obvious — the solution may have far-reaching detrimental consequences that serve to magnify the problem rather than fix it.

Managers, like most other people, have been conditioned to favour the find-an-answer-at-all-costs approach by the education system. The conventional view of reasonably educated people includes a model that suggests: There is one right answer, it can be known and the objective of the exercise is to find it. Ideals like investigation and critical thinking give way to educational pragmatism through rote learning, memorization and reproduction of the singular correct answer retrieved under standardized test conditions.

Yet according to Marshall and Eric McLuhan, the role of education in modern society must have a different objective. The McLuhans observe:

> The goal of science and the arts and of education for the next generation must be to decipher not the genetic but the perceptual code. In a global information environment, the old pattern of education in answer-finding is of no avail ... Survival and control will depend on the ability to probe and to question in the proper way and place. ... [T]he need is not for fixed concepts but rather for ... navigating through an ever uncharted and unchartable milieu.[1]

McLuhan's stated requirement for education would serve business well. If we were all specifically trained and well practiced in probing and questioning —

basic skills required to "decipher … the perceptual code" — the emphasis for solving complex problems would shift from finding the right answer to discovering the right questions. He acknowledges that challenges facing executives as well as managers have become increasingly difficult and non-trivial. McLuhan observes:

> With the acceleration of change, management now takes on entirely new functions. While navigating amidst the unknown is becoming the normal role of the executive, the new need is not merely to navigate but to anticipate effects with their causes.[2]

First, a manager has the task of "navigating amidst the unknown." To further emphasize the primacy of this challenge, McLuhan notes that this is merely "the normal role of the executive." And, as if this is not sufficiently challenging in an age where managers are surrounded by potential alternatives whose number increases at an ever-accelerating pace, a manager must also "anticipate effects with their causes." Let us consider for a moment just how truly daunting are these tasks.

What Business Would You Like to Be in Today? How About Tomorrow?

Consider the objective of "navigating amidst the unknown." When we find ourselves face to face with such a challenge — dealing with the unknown — the typical human response is generally to try something that worked before. However, suppose a manager is told that these are trying times for the company. Things are to be different. Changing times call for changing approaches. It is time to remake — some would say, "re-invent" — the company. It quickly becomes clear to the manager that "what worked before" will not suffice this time. To assist in navigating amidst the unknown, the manager might assemble what he considers to be a brain trust of the department's or company's brightest lights and convene a brainstorming session.

Under the direction of the best facilitator the budget can afford, the team fills flipchart pages with ideas and flashes of insight. The process is often exciting and exhilarating for the participants as one person's creativity and imagination seems to feed on another's. It is the "Perfect Brain Storm": Ideas are tossed this way and that by the power of the creativity deluge that results when several powerful corporate fronts convene and collide. Those participating are whisked along in their enthusiasm for the task, carried about gales of hot, humid air. The outcome is often mixed: At the end, some participants are truly enthusiastic by the promise of the session. Others, perhaps more cynical about the process, may feel frustrated by the results or the direction of the discussions. There may be a few who are simply confused and maybe frightened by the prospects of change.

The critical probe for remaking a company: A company may be in a business, but it may not be the business it is really in.

Experience shows that much of what was accomplished during the brainstorming session will ultimately have little lasting impact or value. Many ideas that arise from these events will prove to be ill-conceived, trivial or unusable in practice. Many will be mere extrapolations or extensions of current business-as-usual. Very few of the ideas, if any, will focus on the critical probe for remaking a company: A company may be in a business, but it may not be the business it is really in.

In *Take Today*, among other places, McLuhan reminds us that all of mankind's utopias are rear-view projections of the recent past.[3] With this probe, he challenges us to think of several different issues. First, it is only in retrospect that we can be sufficiently aware and comfortable with contemplating what happened, as opposed to being able to contemplate what is happening now. Second, as we look back, we will idealize, and sometimes long for, the bygone era. This is the basis of nostalgia. As English poet Lord Byron wrote in *The Age of Bronze*, "The 'good old times' — all times when old are good."[4] By taking the "good old times" and projecting them forward, we conceive of the ideal world — a utopia.

When we envisage the ideal future of our remade business, it is akin to creating the illusion of an ideal world: We project an idealized conception of the company we would have had by now, had we done everything absolutely right, with perfect clarity of vision in the first place. It almost always exists as an extrapolation of the business we think we are in.

It is too easy, and therefore tempting, to simply extrapolate from the current situation when trying to remake a company. Deliver it faster, cheaper, more profitably. Make it in different colours, sizes, packages. Add a twist. Or an olive. Or both. Improve time to market. Reduce inventories. Improve supply chain management. Get closer to the customer. We are the best at what we do. Or, we will become the best at what we do. We are the biggest, the first, the fastest.

The problem is that extrapolation does not remake a company. This process of extension literally looks at the recent past — the rear view — and idealizes it, projecting it forward into our corporate utopia, writ large upon our market. So, for example, the telecommunications company that manages networks so well in its long-haul data transport business, decides that it will strategically emphasize the managed networks market. It "remakes" itself from a company that is a leader in managing networks to one that has ambitions to be a leader in managed networks, that is, managing networks for others. Same *ground*: High technology telecommunications industry selling to technical buyers, who are increasingly putting more weight on a financially-based decision criteria. Same *figure*: Network management technology and expertise, emphasizing reliability, availability and depth of experience. So what's new? The logo, slogan and ad campaign.

The problem is that extrapolation does not remake a company.

Naturally, a company must continue to do what it has done to sustain itself and its revenue flow. But if the ultimate destination is one of "remaking the company," the first step on that journey is to become aware. Those charged with architecting the remade company must first perceive the current *ground* as it truly is now, not as it once was. For example, the telecommunications company's *ground* may have shifted so that it has become more of a commodity market, rather than a technology market *per se*. Perceiving this could allow strategists to contemplate the company as a new Medium, one that has different effects on its market. In other words, the remade company would — should — have a different Message.

Carefully considering whether the business *ground* has changed helps avoid an all too common mistake — attempting to remake the company by emulating the market-leading competitor, or the market leader in a new market. Putting on someone else's clothing does not change you into the someone else: A corporate sheep dressed as the market wolf will still get eaten!

A corporate sheep
dressed as the
market wolf will
still get eaten!

IBM and Compaq

For instance, a company facing a declining market and fierce competition may choose to remake itself by assuming the image of a successful, market-leading company in order to quickly enter a new market. A hardware manufacturer may decide to become a solutions provider or services company, for example. Think of IBM and Compaq. In both cases, a nominal hardware manufacturer, faced with fierce competition from new markets watches helplessly as its business declines according to almost every measure — revenue, earnings growth, market share, unit sales and so forth.

In the early 1990s, IBM faced tremendous competitive pressure in its core mainframe business, both from direct competitors Amdahl and Hitachi Data Systems, as well as from indirect alternative-platform competitors offering Unix-based servers and client-server applications. IBM remade itself into a solutions provider, becoming relatively agnostic about hardware and software platforms — a first for the technology colossus. Within a very few years, it bounced back to its former glory as a formidable competitor, a dominant force in its new market.[5]

Similarly, Compaq found itself losing significant market share in its core personal computer workstation and server businesses. Part of the decline was due to direct competitive pressures from the likes of Dell Computer Corporation and Hewlett-Packard. But the nature of business acquisitions of such equipment changed as well: The majority of business workstations and servers were being bought as part of larger systems solutions involving consulting and large-scale software development and implementation, often provided by companies such as EDS and IBM.[6]

In its attempt to remake itself, Compaq decided to enter the enterprise solutions market by "putting on the clothing" of market leader, IBM. It bought the former Digital Equipment Corporation for both its server-oriented hardware assets — the Alpha chip technology — and its expertise in providing technology solutions. The result was not entirely as anticipated: The Alpha technology did not win market acceptance and was sold to Intel for short-term income gain. After several failed attempts to enter the software market, the search engine market and the vertical industry solutions market, Compaq remained a ship adrift in the shark-infested technology sea, until Hewlett-Packard, another technology vessel facing similar adversity, came to its apparent rescue via a bitterly fought merger, whose success is as yet unknown.[7]

The difference between IBM and Compaq is that, for the second time in IBM's history, its leaders had a unique awareness and perception of their company and the effects it creates for its customers. Simply put, IBM's senior management realized that they were not actually in the business they nominally believed they were in. IBM in the 1950s sold business equipment. Management eventually recognized that while IBM was nominally in business equipment, it actually was in the information processing business. With information processing as its focus, IBM enjoyed market dominance and tremendous growth for nearly forty years.

When the market shifted, IBM's leaders at the time were caught in the "*figure* recedes into *ground*" hypnosis. In other words, IBM's former business tactics, modes of operation and success were almost taken for granted, more as context themselves, rather than as issues to be considered relative to a context of market realities. This resulted in a 75 percent loss in market value that nearly ruined the company in the first half of the 1990s.

While remedial action was taken to stem the losses, the new leadership brought in from outside — Louis Gerstner and his team — set out to remake IBM according to the business it was really in, as opposed to its nominal business. The new senior management were not hampered by the "hidden *ground*" as were their predecessors. Gerstner undertook a massive and disruptive restructuring effort to recast IBM explicitly as a global solutions provider, something that it had been doing, to a greater or lesser extent, for years. Focused on this new *figure*, the company's fortunes were reversed, much to the delight of shareholders and customers alike.[8]

Disruption, Dat Ruption...

The requirement for noticeable disruption when attempting to remake a company should not be underestimated. In most cases where an action as

Any innovation threatens the equilibrium of existing organization. Therefore, no new idea starts from within a big operation. Understanding Media, 1964

The requirement for noticeable disruption when attempting to remake a company should not be underestimated.

drastic as remaking is needed, the company's context has invariably become a hidden *ground*, unnoticed by most of the company's management and staff. The company's effects on its market, customers and others become less evident as they recede into the *ground* and take on the characteristics of assumptions as opposed to explicit observations. In McLuhanistic terms, the company's Message is lost, and therefore, so is the Medium — the company itself.

Merely attempting to introduce new ideas is insufficient, as companies tend to protect themselves against such changes. McLuhan cynically observes:

> Any innovation threatens the equilibrium of existing organization. In big industry new ideas are invited to rear their heads so that they can be clobbered at once. ... Such [an idea] would be a disaster for the existing management. They would have to make way for new management. Therefore, no new idea starts from within a big operation.[9]

Chris Argyris, the James B. Conant Professor at the Harvard Graduate School of Business, wrote about the mechanisms by which individual managers and organizations defend themselves against noticeably disruptive ideas and changes. In his article, "Good Communication That Blocks Learning,"[10] Argyris describes the difference between how individuals intend to behave versus how they actually behave in difficult situations. The latter, which he calls one's "theory-in-use," describes behaviours that individuals use "in order to remain in unilateral control, to maximize winning and minimize losing, to suppress negative feelings, and to be as rational as possible..."[11]

On the surface, these motivations may appear to be reasonable. Argyris notes, however, that, "the purpose of this strategy is to avoid vulnerability, risk, embarrassment, and the appearance of incompetence. ... [I]t helps us avoid reflecting on the counterproductive consequences of our own behaviour."[12] Similar behaviours, that he calls "organizational defensive routines" occur systemically, consisting of "all the policies, practices, and actions that prevent human beings from having to experience embarrassment or threat and, at the same time, prevent them from examining the nature and causes of that embarrassment or threat."[13]

New ideas that are potentially threatening to managers or to the organization, that is, those that would cause noticeable disruption, activate the defensive mechanisms that Argyris describes in his article. However, by understanding the corporation as a Medium relative to its *ground*, we have a relatively less threatening way of examining the nature of problems, opportunities and potential approaches. Becoming aware of the company's current *ground* allows managers to carefully examine how its context has changed and begin to consider how to respond.

Originally, a company is created on the basis of certain business assumptions that define its context: Market conditions, the general economy, potential customers' needs and buying processes, availability of particular expertise and capabilities, among other things, all contribute to the context. But these, of necessity, change over time. In fact, the company itself is responsible for many of the changes according to the McLuhan Equation, the Medium is the Message. The company has effected change by its interactions and relationships with its market, customers, staff and the economy in general. The *ground* has changed. We also know that these changes have, in turn, changed the company through the mechanism of feedforward, although it is likely that management and many staff would not have the awareness and perception to be able to observe it from within.

McLuhanistic insight gives managers a way to understand the nature and effects of the company-as-Medium. It becomes a non-threatening means whereby they can develop sets of expectations of what might occur and what effects may be seen when new ideas are introduced relative to the changed *ground*. While not exactly deterministic prediction, looking at the company-as-Medium casts the problem of looking ahead into the unknown as one of attempting to anticipate likely effects.

Effects and Causes

The manager now comes face to face with McLuhan's second challenge to executives: "... not merely to navigate but to anticipate effects with

"Causes become effects via concepts, whereas effects merge with causes in process pattern recognition via percepts." Take Today: The Executive as Dropout, 1972

their causes."[14] What is particularly interesting about this expression is that we typically think of the cliché of "cause and effect" — some event is causal, and therefore it results in an effect. McLuhan has sharpened this into an important cliché-probe. With the phrase, "effects with their causes," he reminds us that Media do not act linearly, with causes preceding effects in lockstep fashion. Rather, Media exist, and by their very existence introduce changes by way of their Message — the effects. However, the effects themselves are not linear. In fact, they exhibit more non-linear, network-like characteristics as effects fan out and touch all with whom the company interacts.

We experience the effects directly — they result in perceptions. On the

The awareness of many possible effects allows corporate managers to antici-pate useful causes.

other hand, causes are conceptions — mental models that allow us to match perceptions to patterns that we carry in our minds. The notion of causes helps us to understand and rationalize a Medium's perceived effects in order to make them useful in a particular context. When a manager first becomes aware of a Medium's effects, it does not mean that the effects are inevitable. Rather, the awareness of many possible effects allows corporate managers to anticipate useful causes, that is, to manage business activities in such a manner that the *desired* effects occur with respect to the appropriate *ground*.

Understanding the nature of the Messages, that is, the effects and changes, is the way to understand Media — the extensions of man that are our innovations, technologies and ideas. Or, as McLuhan succinctly puts it, "Invention is the mother of necessity."[15]

Inventing Necessity

An idea when expressed through some mechanism is a Medium, representing an extension of human ability. Its value lies in its Message, that is, what change in scale, pace or pattern will be spawned by the idea, and how that change will affect those whom it touches. Conventionally, when a manager contemplates innovative changes that may enable certain new facilities or capabilities, he or she considers the effects they may have on the company relative to its objectives. The change may save time and money. It may increase revenue or allow tasks to be performed quicker or easier. The company may introduce capabilities and facilities that can revolutionize business processes and practices for its customers. This would allow them to reap the benefits of "quicker and cheaper."

Enabling capabilities such as these are often regarded as the benefits or upsides of the proposed changes. Proponents of these ideas will always be able to answer the question "How does this idea extend the company's capabilities to our, and our customers', advantage?" They may, for example, come up with conventional explanations, such as, lowering cost of production will allow us to lower prices and thereby become more competitive. Repackaging a current offering will allow us to sell into a previously unavailable market segment. Implementing just-in-time inventory management will allow us to reduce the carrying expense and warehousing costs associated with managing stockpiles of raw materials and subassemblies.

Persuasive proponents of almost any new idea can conjure up sufficient benefits to make their position seem compelling. However, supporters of the idea must reckon with the adversarial dynamics and Argyris' "organizational defensive routines" that exist in most corporations. As is often the case, if an idea's proponent acknowledges a point of view that somehow diminishes an anticipated benefit, it is seen as weakening his position, and thereby causes embarrassment. Naturally, this perception encourages managers to primarily focus on the extensions and benefits of ideas to the exclusion of any other consideration. Naysayers are often accused of being negative and reminded, "We're all on the same team here."

Online Shopping

Consider the business aspects of shopping online via the World Wide Web. The benefits offered by such businesses are clear. By allowing busy consumers to shop from their workstations at home or at work, at any time of the day or night, shopping convenience hits a new high. No longer would consumers have to jostle with fellow last-minute Christmas present hunters. A few clicks of the mouse and the week's groceries would be bought,

Naysayers are often accused of being negative and reminded, "We're all on the same team here."

birthday presents shipped, and the summer's reading material would be on the way in time for vacation.

The ubiquitous availability of pricing information from retailers around the world and on auction sites means that lowest prices for any commodity imaginable would be virtually assured. If one was so inclined, at one time, even luxury items such as fine jewellery, *objets d'art*, expensive vehicles and rare vacation properties were available for purchase online. Comparison shopping was, again, merely a click away. Services sprung up that provided automated comparison pricing by searching the shopping sites and consolidating price quotes. As one might expect, meta-services emerged that evaluated the relative capabilities of price-comparison sites. And, there was convenient home or office delivery to boot!

Online shopping possessed the perfect recipe for success. The problem was that it was not ultimately successful as a business.

Convenience, lowest prices and delivery are compelling consumer benefits. Online shopping could not possibly fail. In fact, many boosters and industry pundits preached "disintermediation" — the elimination of middlemen in business and retail transactions. Online shopping possessed the perfect recipe for success. Such were the efficiencies achievable in a "frictionless information economy."

The only problem was that online Web-based shopping was not ultimately successful as a business in its own right. Simply put, the business model was loosely based on the old joke about losing money on each transaction but making it up in volume. The obvious benefits to consumers were indeed convenience, price and delivery. Companies convinced themselves that with the availability of instantaneous information, traditional old-economy expenses like conventional advertising, distributors, maintaining substantial inventories and so forth could be eliminated, thereby reducing operating cost. Few counted on the increased expense associated with building substantial technological infrastructures to support the resulting volumes. Delivery costs were grossly underestimated — new economy denizens thought it was great entertainment to have a single Snickers bar delivered by scooter to their downtown desk. Capital expenditure associated with building distribution centres and warehouses far exceeded expectations and eliminated economic efficiencies that would be obtained through Internet-based information flow. The cost of handling errors, returns and the unexpectedly large contingent of disgruntled customers never found its way into wildly optimistic business plans.

Ultimately, getting timely supply, maintaining inventory, delivery and overall logistics proved to be both too expensive and too consumptive of inexperienced management's time. As it turned out, the old rules seemed to apply in a new economy — the clear ability to make a profit is a required cost of doing business. Countless numbers of investors, would-be entrepreneurs and ordinary workers collectively lost billions of dollars, simply because it was only the beneficial aspects of the new businesses that were considered. The benefits were compelling, but no one considered aspects of the Message other than, "What are the upsides and advantages of the changes?" No one considered the full range of changes and effects that e-businesses would cause in the context of the larger economy, human behaviour and society in general.

Clearly, through the rear-view mirror, we can easily identify what were the possible downsides or risks. From the perspective of driving by the wreckage dragged to the side of the once vaunted information highway, it is easy to cluck our tongues and enumerate those changes in pace and scale that would have obviously predicted the inevitable outcome. Any manager today can easily point a finger and say, "They should have known better…"

Of course they should have. But the truth is, that among thousands of seasoned business people and investors who watched helplessly as tremendous wealth in their tech-heavy portfolios vaporized over less than a year, few did know better. They eagerly sought the upside, but ignored the downside. The upside of online shopping eliminated time, high prices and the consumer's requirement for travel — all benefits. At its conception, online shopping significantly reduced fixed overhead. However, the accompanying downside meant that marginal, incremental profit was also reduced as the variable overhead cost components of each transaction dominated. The online marketplace meant that competitors were literally a click away, reducing customer loyalty and the advantage of physical presence. This, in turn, reduced avail-

Today, the business of business is becoming the constant invention of new business. Take Today: The Executive as Dropout, 1972

INTRODUCING A NEW CRYSTAL BALL

ability of incremental margins that are traditionally achieved by up-selling higher margin items to loyal customers who are already in the store.

These turned out to be very real disadvantages to online retail business. If those making business decisions concerning possible investments in these ventures were to have considered the upside, the downside and what was eliminated or reduced, a far more insightful investment decision could have been made.

There is one further aspect to consider. To gain yet another perspective on their proposed businesses, prospective entrepreneurs might have asked themselves, "Does this new economy e-business remind us of anything?" Most of the online shopping revolution was really nothing more than old style, mail order catalogue shopping hyped up with new style e-mail. Taking lessons from successful catalogue operations would have revealed valuable management and operational insights. These views could have provided the requisite illumination of the business realities about to be faced.

Initially, it may seem somewhat simplistic to believe that all can be revealed by answering four questions: What is the upside, what is the downside, what is eliminated and where have we seen this before? However, it is not simply the questions themselves, but the mind-opening thought processes that these probes initiate that are of significance and provide the needed illumination.

There is one minor problem with looking at things using the labels of "upside" and "downside." These terms convey a value judgement that may or may not be justified, depending on the context. Upsides are generally considered beneficial and are often the extensions or enabling characteristics of a Medium's Message. Conversely, downsides are often considered negatively as risks or deleterious effects inadvertently or unavoidably introduced by the effected change. However, as we are attempting to understand the nature of the Medium, it is important that we stay away from value judgements early in the process.

Our complete understanding of a new Medium and its effects depends on expanding our thinking and insights. By self-editing or filtering, possibly valuable ideas that could lead to breakthrough insights would be eliminated. As McLuhan once wrote in correspondence with a critic, "Value judgments create smog in our culture and distract attention from processes."[16] In order to properly focus on the processes — the effects — of a Medium, McLuhan's structure presupposes no judgement about the relative value of any of its inherent effects.

The Laws of Media

Marshall and Eric McLuhan postulate four Laws of Media. They maintain the laws apply without exception to all creations of humankind, whether tangible or intangible, abstract or concrete. They also claim that there are *precisely* four laws that reveal the nature of any Medium, and they challenge readers to find an example that possesses only three attributes, or a fifth that applies in every case. Not surprisingly, the Laws of Media are framed as questions or probes:

> **The Laws of Media are framed as questions or probes.**

- What does the artefact enhance or intensify or make possible or accelerate? This can be asked concerning a wastebasket, a painting, a steamroller, or a zipper, as well as about a proposition in Euclid or a law of physics. It can be asked about any word or phrase in any language.

- If some aspect of a situation is enlarged or enhanced, simultaneously the old condition or unenhanced situation is displaced thereby. What is pushed aside or obsolesced by the new "organ"?

- What recurrence or retrieval of earlier actions and services is brought into play simultaneously by the new form? What older, previously obsolesced ground is brought back and inheres in the new form?

- When pushed to the limits of its potential (another complementary action), the new form will tend to reverse what had been its original characteristics. What is the reversal potential of the new form?[17]

Extend. Obsolesce. Retrieve. Reverse. All of these effects occur in the Medium at once, simultaneously. It is not that one or the other occurs at different times, nor does one cause or lead to another. All of the effects are present and reflect the systemic nature of the effects of a Medium: They all act together, affecting us and other Media with which the given Medium interacts. This is, admittedly, a difficult concept to grasp at first, but it is another manifestation of the phenomenon of all-at-onceness that we discussed in the first chapter.

To emphasize this unity of effects, McLuhan arranges the probes as four quadrants of a tetrad:[18]

MEDIUM

What does the medium EXTEND, enhance, enable or intensify?

When extended beyond its limits into what does the medium REVERSE?

What formerly obsolesced form does the medium RETRIEVE from the past?

What does the medium OBSOLESCE?

For the Laws of Media tetrads to serve their purpose as probes into the nature of any Medium, it is important to remember that McLuhan eschewed rules and rigidity in his thinking process. For example, the dividing lines illustrated in the tetrad above and those to follow are typographical conveniences only; McLuhan himself disapproved of them.

Applying the Laws of Media can sometimes be challenging and requires some practice. Let us begin by constructing Laws of Media tetrads for a few simple examples from our everyday, working world, starting with the pen. What follows could be characterized as a stream of consciousness that results from beginning with one perception of the pen's effects, and allowing the other simultaneous Laws of Media aspects to emerge.

The ballpoint or roller-ball pen, with its self-contained, long-lasting reservoir of ink, EXTENDS continuous writing time by eliminating — OBSOLESCING — the need for dipping a nib-style pen into ink. The Message of this Medium, that is, the change that such a capability effects, is the ability to EXTEND our expression of continuous thought, without pauses. However, when such expression is EXTENDED beyond a reasonable limit, free expression REVERSES INTO verbosity, and possibly physical cramping of the hand that holds the pen. Compared to a modern pen, the pauses necessitated by the OBSOLESCED nib-style or archaic quill pen forced periodic interruptions in the flow of thought, which promoted contemplation and mental reflection. With the continuously flowing pen, these are OBSOLESCED. In not requiring periodic refills to enable writing, the pen RETRIEVES one aspect of the ancient stylus on clay.

Because of its relative portability and longevity, the pen OBSOLESCES reliance on memory to record thoughts and notes, enabling accurate reporting of quotations, impressions and incidents. Such accuracy RETRIEVES the notion of scribes, whose responsibility it was to accurately record the events of the day, the chronicles of royalty or decrees of the land.

An ability to do something often makes a transition in a person's mind become an obligation.

As continuity of thought is EXTENDED, so too is the ability for continuous writing. However, an ability to do something often makes a transition in a person's mind become an obligation — in this case, a tacit obligation on the part of the writer to be expressive and write. Ironically, as most professional writers will attest, this subtle, often self-imposed, pressure may result in writer's block, the REVERSAL of continuous writing and expression. Often, when a writer is blocked, he will resort to "doodling," or drawing meaningless sketches or pictures around the page; this RETRIEVES the artistic nature of writing, reminiscent of medieval scribes who often embellished their scrolls with highly artistic illustrations.

The resulting tetrad looks like this:

PEN

EXTENDS

⋯⟩ Writing time

⋯⟩ Continuity of thought (by eliminating interruptions for refilling)

⋯⟩ Recollection, quotation (by enabling note-taking)

REVERSES INTO

⋯⟩ "Doodling," the artist's brush

⋯⟩ Writer's cramp

⋯⟩ Verbosity

⋯⟩ Writer's block

RETRIEVES

⋯⟩ Stylus on clay tablet

⋯⟩ Writing as art form, calligraphy, penmanship

⋯⟩ Scribes

OBSOLESCES

⋯⟩ Nib-style pen (or quill) and ink

⋯⟩ Memory

⋯⟩ Mental reflection, contemplation

With such a simple device as the modern pen, it is almost surprising to discover how many Messages are revealed through a quickly constructed Laws of Media tetrad. One might reasonably query the relevance of performing this analysis on a pen. However, for the marketing manager of Bic or Pentel, for example, these insights may well spur creativity and inspiration that will ultimately seed a new product or marketing thrust.

As we went through the various items, we observed the pen's action or effect and then thought about complementary actions. As we noted earlier, there is no particular order in which the various aspects come within our field of awareness.

Likewise, there is no linear progression of one aspect to the next. Rather, awareness, perception and insight come into focus as we allow our minds to make connections and recognize patterns of effects.

Learning from History

Here is another example of the Laws of Media tetrad for something found in almost every office: the photocopier.

PHOTOCOPIER

EXTENDS

···⟩ Pen

···⟩ Process of duplication

···⟩ Communication of (written) ideas

···⟩ Self-publishing

···⟩ Freedom of expression, freedom of the press

REVERSES INTO

···⟩ Plagiarism, copyright infringement

···⟩ Vanity publishing

···⟩ Propaganda, distribution of controversial material

···⟩ Controlling the agenda (by fixing, printing and distributing the agenda in advance)

RETRIEVES

···⟩ Gutenberg's movable type

···⟩ Underground and independent press

···⟩ Multipartite participation in issues (through receiving copies in advance)

OBSOLESCES

···⟩ Older methods of copying, e.g. ditto, carbon paper, hand copying, etc.

···⟩ Editorial oversight

···⟩ Censorship

Again, we see there are some items in several quadrants that are relatively obvious, and some less so. Sometimes, one attribute will suggest an entire category of thought investigation because of its intrinsic richness as a Medium itself. In this case, for example, the photocopier RETRIEVES the notion of Johannes Gutenberg's fifteenth century movable type. Movable type subsequently led to the invention of the printing press, resulting in the vast mechanization of writing and wide distribution of printed materials. As McLuhan describe throughout his many books, mechanized printing engendered nothing less than an explosive revolution in society. He drew direct effect and cause links between the printing press and standardization of national languages and the subsequent rise of nationalism and nationalist movements. Literacy became a measure of individual worth and status. Linearity, uniformity and continuity in form and thought shaped literature, philosophy, architecture and design for centuries.

When one considers the impact of a RETRIEVED item that itself has historical significance, like the RETRIEVAL of Gutenberg's movable type, it is only natural to consider whether the new Medium under consideration might have similarly important effects. By reflecting on the RETRIEVAL quadrant as one that introduces precedents, we may be able to glean valuable clues as to the effects of the new Medium from the more easily observed effects of the old. Are there applications for the now ubiquitous photocopier outside of simply making copies? More important, when the photocopier reached the height of its popularity, would such wider, thought-expanding considerations have enabled even greater use of the device and its wider distribution? As a simple example, if the printing press's historical ability for distributing ideas was extended as *figure*, against the *ground* of photocopier technology, "Xerox" as verb may have become as synonymous with "fax" as it is with photocopying.

Many aspects revealed in the Laws of Media tetrad work by suggesting analogies that provoke deeper, non-obvious thinking. Sometimes random thoughts connect metaphorically, transforming a conception of the Medium being investigated into a completely new

Retrieval always seems to provide the dominant mode of each tetrad, which may explain why it is often the most difficult to discover. Laws of Media: The New Science, 1988

realization. The newly discovered effects could then enable us to consider the Medium in an entirely new light.

An example of this is the photocopier extending freedom of speech and expression. Using metaphors in thinking about the Messages of new Media is an important vehicle for bringing the experience of our *ground* — the business context — to bear on the problem of how the Medium will affect those whom it touches. Consider McLuhan's probe of poet Robert Browning:

> "A man's reach must exceed his grasp, else what's a metaphor?" All media are active metaphors in their power to translate experience into new forms. The spoken word was the first technology by which man was able to let go of his environment in order to grasp it in a new way.[19]

In the case of the sharpened Browning cliché-probe, "reach" and "grasp" are themselves used metaphorically. Naturally, McLuhan is referring to mental reach and grasp — our ability to use language to conceive of new effects, perhaps never before seen or experienced. When he says that we "let go of our environment," McLuhan is referring to our personal environment, and our direct experience, hampered by limited awareness. Language — especially metaphors — allows us "to grasp it [understand our environment] in a new way," with increased awareness. Using the four Laws spurs this creativity of thought and encourages grasping at new metaphors. Mental freedom and creativity, in turn, allow us to understand and anticipate potential effects on our metaphorical environment — that is, our selves and our immediate experiences — that a new Medium will have.

We are the context — the environment — within which Media act and cause change. By probing the effects of various Media in the appropriate context, we begin to gain the ability to explicitly understand how we might react to the Medium, the ways in which it may change us, and how it and other Media could evolve in response. Businesses now gain a valuable way to understand possible future effects, implications, likelihood of success and potential repercussions of new offerings and initiatives.

Let us try one more example, working step by step from Marshall McLuhan's own *ground*. Of all the new Media he considered, the most fascinating for Marshall McLuhan during his lifetime may have been the computer for the sheer potential of its Message. As early as 1967 McLuhan observed that, "electric circuitry [is] an extension of the central nervous system."[20]

In this quotation, we have McLuhan's first metaphorical EXTENSION of the computer: It EXTENDS our central nervous system. What is interesting in this comment is that he views the central nervous system — our internal communications network — and not the brain itself as being EXTENDED. He also notes in *Laws of Media* that, "The computer speeds calculation and retrieval, obsolescing the 'Bob Cratchit' bookkeepers."[21] Our first tetrad iteration is then:

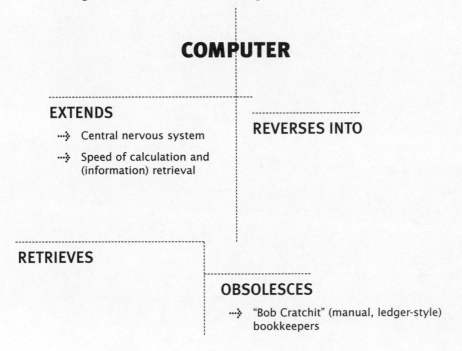

COMPUTER

EXTENDS

⋯⋗ Central nervous system

⋯⋗ Speed of calculation and (information) retrieval

REVERSES INTO

RETRIEVES

OBSOLESCES

⋯⋗ "Bob Cratchit" (manual, ledger-style) bookkeepers

By speeding or EXTENDING information retrieval from electronic and magnetic storage, computers diminish and eventually OBSOLESCE the need for physically published reference materials and the physical buildings in which they are housed. Witness, for example, the decline of the expensively bound, printed encyclopedia, and other reference works. The authoritative *Encyclopaedia Britannica*, which once retailed for over $1,000 is now available on CD-ROM, with instant keyword indexing, for under $50. Unfortunately, the *Britannica* publishers were late to understand the implications of the Message and lost significant market share. Microsoft, on the other hand, intimately understood the potential of the Medium. It purchased the rights to Funk and Wagnall's — popularized as the brunt of jokes by *Laugh In*, a television comedy/satire show in the 1970s — and launched it as *Microsoft Encarta*, breathing life into the CD-ROM encyclopedia market.

With instant, central retrieval of information, the computer reminds one of the wise elder, or an electronic version of same. Of course, unlike human memory, with electronic storage there is perfection of recall. We may be tempted to jump to the conclusion that this means that the computer's recall is total, complete and accurate. This would suggest an EXTENSION of the authority of stored information, a phenomenon often observed in the additional credence given to a computer-generated, printed report, or the Internet as an authoritative source.

However, even though this suggestion would tend to OBSOLESCE human memory, the computer's recall is only as accurate and complete as its source of programming and data entry. As the saying goes, if you put garbage in, you get garbage out. When trust in the electronic authority is EXTENDED beyond a reasonable degree, we may fall prey to hoaxes and misinformation.

Perhaps one of the most damaging examples of this effect of the computer was demonstrated — if not provoked — by the theory presented in *Limits to Growth*.[22] This 1973 best seller claimed — with much conjectural and statistical evidence to support it — that the world economy was heading to a rapid end for lack of renewable resources. The conjectural evidence, it so happens, was obtained by the much improved simulations and calculations afforded by the then latest computers. De Kerckhove attempted to explain elsewhere that what actually provoked the deep recession of the 1970s was yet another example of how the Medium is the Message.[23]

What actually provoked the deep recession of the 1970s was yet another example of how the Medium is the Message.

The trigger that started the doomsday scenario developed in *Limits to Growth* was a report by the respected economist Herman Kahn from the Hudson Institute, produced with the help of a mainframe computer. The machine's rapid calculations enabled him to generate enough dire predictions about the natural limits of our natural resources to chill any investor. The futility of those predictions, especially the ones concerning the soon-to-be depleted world oil reserves, was demonstrated in 1976. After three years of brutal recession owing to the fears engendered by the imminence of oil scarcity, the oil-consuming countries unexpectedly faced an oil glut.

The real cause of this change of mood from a psychology of affluence coming out of the 1960s to one of recession in the 1970s was not oil, but the effect of, and misplaced credence given to, the latest technology on the block — the computer.

Our tetrad has now evolved to:

COMPUTER

EXTENDS

- ···⟩ Central nervous system
- ···⟩ Speed of calculation and (information) retrieval
- ···⟩ Authority of stored information

REVERSES INTO

- ···⟩ Hoaxes, misinformation
- ···⟩ "Garbage in, garbage out"
- ···⟩ Overreliance on one information source to the exclusion of others

RETRIEVES

- ···⟩ Wise elder
- ···⟩ Perfection of recall
  Total, complete, accurate

OBSOLESCES

- ···⟩ "Bob Cratchit" (manual, ledger-style) bookkeepers
- ···⟩ Bound, printed encyclopedias and other reference works
- ···⟩ Physical libraries
- ···⟩ Human memory
- ···⟩ Judgement

If we think about McLuhan's notion of the computer as an EXTENSION of our central nervous system, we may contemplate its role in interconnecting all of our sensory inputs — the sources of external information. Often, one sense enhances another by virtue of all being interconnected. For example, when presented with a meal, the senses of sight, taste and smell all work in tandem to produce an experience that is more than any of the individual senses could provide alone. It is well established, for instance, that our concept of flavour is the effect of both smell and taste.

Overloading one sense may de-emphasize another. For instance, being visually distracted by an attractive person often diminishes one's ability to listen. Overloading one sense to the extreme may cause it to fail — think of standing near the amplified speakers at a rock concert. If all senses are overloaded, the entire nervous system, including the brain itself, may protectively shut down into unconsciousness.

In the case of information overload, our ability to comprehend each additional piece of information declines rapidly. Hence, we quickly become unable to treat information as discrete items to be processed and assimilated sequentially. Information overload often throws us into a state of chaos. However, in response, we may begin to perceive that patterns emerge from the chaotic mass of information. Rather than conventional linear thinking, we consciously begin to move toward pattern recognition, from which, incidentally, often comes new insights.

Notice in this discussion how we used physical sensory reactions as metaphors to enable new thinking. We transformed "sensory overload" into "information overload," which led us to "pattern recognition." You are welcome to EXTEND your own thinking about pattern recognition into possible ways in which to manage your personal information overload challenges. In the meantime, we can add these insights to the computer's tetrad as follows:

All meaning alters with acceleration, because all patterns ... change with any acceleration of information. *Understanding Media*, 1964

COMPUTER

EXTENDS

---> Central nervous system

---> Speed of calculation and (information) retrieval

---> Authority of stored information

---> Sources of information

---> Connectivity and consolidation of information

REVERSES INTO

---> Hoaxes, misinformation

---> "Garbage in, garbage out"

---> Over-reliance on one information source to the exclusion of others

---> Network failure, lack of communications, isolation

---> Information overload ---> pattern recognition

RETRIEVES

---> Wise elder

---> Perfection of recall
Total, complete, accurate

OBSOLESCES

---> "Bob Cratchit" (manual, ledger-style) bookkeepers

---> Bound, printed encyclopedias and other reference works

---> Physical libraries

---> Human memory

---> Judgement

McLuhan goes one step further when considering the computer as an EXTENSION of the central nervous system. He contemplates the following extremely EXTENDED possibility as probe: "Having extended or translated our central nervous system into the electromagnetic technology, it is but a further stage to transfer our consciousness to the computer world as well."[24] If we (metaphorically) EXTEND our consciousness to the computer — one that is interconnected by a network serving as the world's central nervous system — we can envision people storing and sharing their thoughts and experiences, and communicating without boundaries or limitations at any time. We can perhaps even conceive of virtual places in which our avatars interact with one another, developing relationships and living lives quite apart from our physical existence. While not exactly "transferring our consciousness to the computer," the Internet of the 2000s is a remarkable prediction to have been made from the perspective of 1964.

As we mentioned earlier, the power of the four Media Laws lies in their ability to encourage all-at-once contemplation of both the nature and effects of a Medium under consideration. This occurs because of the underlying principles of the *Laws of Media*:

> This tetrad of the effects of technologies and artefacts presents not a sequential process, but rather four simultaneous ones. All four aspects are inherent in each artefact from the start. The four aspects are complementary, and require careful observation of the artefact in relation to its ground, rather than consideration in the abstract.[25]

There is no sequence to discovering the aspects. The Medium does not first EXTEND, then REVERSE, then OBSOLESCE and finally RETRIEVE. At the same time that the Medium EXTENDS some capability, it simultaneously OBSOLESCES some older form or Medium, while RETRIEVING a previously OBSOLESCED *ground*. If the Medium is EXTENDED too far, it will REVERSE INTO another complementary form that may be desirable, undesirable or neutral with respect to our impression of it.

All of these aspects exist simultaneously and exist instantly at the moment of the Medium's creation or conception. However, we may not become instantly aware of certain aspects. That may take years. This also does not mean that every aspect that describes the Medium or its Message for all time comes into existence at that moment. As a Medium changes, so too do its various aspects. A Medium is not static in its nature, action or effect. Remember that as we react to the changes caused by the Medium and are changed by its Message, we cannot help but change our perception of it. The same applies to our judgement of its Message. These myriad subtle changes begin to shift the *ground* and thereby the context or environment within which we interact with the Medium and understand its effects. Therefore, the Medium cannot be considered in the abstract, but rather as a *figure* with respect to its specific *ground* at the time.

A Medium is not static in its nature, action or effect.

Because of this, there are potentially an infinite number of possible tetrads for a given Medium over time. The user provides the context. Each person who considers the Medium will approach it from a unique perspective. Within a relatively large context, a marketing department considering a new product, for example, a relatively consistent tetrad would likely be constructed. But for multiple, distinct contexts, a consolidated tetrad may result in a hodgepodge of aspects, metaphors, effects and possible changes, each of which is valid with respect to someone's *ground*.

Consider, for example, members of a marketing department applying the Laws of Media to a new product, and those in human resources doing the same thing. Each will undoubtedly develop unique tetrads, as each has a unique perspective, context and environment. We cannot ask which is right. Rather, we can use a more incisive probe: "Which *is*?" That is, which *figure/ground* combination best describes the appropriate in-context perception for the circumstances? By "appropriate" we mean the context in which the Medium will act on a particular segment or aspect of the business environment.

We must listen to our instinct and draw on our life experience to understand the changes that are possible with a Medium.

A Medium cannot be understood in the abstract, or in the context of an arbitrarily imposed, idealized view of reality. A Medium acts on us in the here and now, or if you would prefer, the *hear and know*. We must listen to our instinct and draw on our life experience to understand the changes that are possible with a Medium. We then can look forward and ask the quintessentially McLuhanesque probe, "…and what will that change?"

⋯⋯⋮⟩ For use almost can change the stamp of nature, and either master the devil, or throw him out with wondrous potency.

William Shakespeare, *The Tragedy of Hamlet, Prince of Denmark*

5. Through the GLASS DA

"It is only on those terms, standing

RKLY

aside from any structure or medium,

that its principles and lines of

force

can be discerned. For any medium has the

power

of imposing its own assumption on the unwary."

—Understanding Media, 1964

Despite the best intentions and efforts of an army of experts, analysts and consultants, their recommendations are limited by the questions they are able to ask. Paradoxically, our conventional understanding of new things ultimately seems to be restricted to the information of which we have prior knowledge. In other words, we can only know what we already know, or know about. Business leaders could legitimately ask their advisors, "How do we know that all the right questions have been asked? How can we know what it is we *don't* know?"

The Laws of Media provide us with exactly four questions by which we can begin to understand the nature and effects of all Media — all inventions, products, services, ideas, plans or strategies. These questions collectively refer to characteristics that exist simultaneously in the Medium and relate to one another. Although there are only four questions, there are always many answers. Each set of answers is dependent on a *ground* or context that is specific to the individual answering the questions, or the general environment within which the Medium exists and acts.

In much the same way that a poem might have a rhyme scheme across four-line stanzas, the Laws of Media have correspondences among their four aspects. In the poem, there may be a pattern of similar sounds between individual lines that join as couplets. There may also be an overall rhyming pattern among the four lines taken as a group, providing a structure that repeats in each stanza.

Rather than the similar sounds in a rhyme, the tetrads have similar and complementary concepts or themes among their four quadrants. For example, a Medium may EXTEND a particular characteristic or enhance a specific capability. When that particular item is EXTENDED beyond reasonable limits, the over-extension REVERSES into a complementary, but opposite action or form that directly and thematically corresponds to the specific EXTENSION. Similarly, the EXTENDED offering would OBSOLESCE some attribute of an earlier Medium that relates to the aspect being EXTENDED, and RETRIEVE an earlier form of that aspect belonging to some previously OBSOLESCED Medium.

As will be illustrated in this chapter, when the tetrad is complete, or rather, has been investigated as far as insightful thinking allows, patterns of "sub-tetrads" become evident. Some may think of them as being closer to a fractal instance of the tetrad, in that each smaller set has the same structure as the tetrad in its entirety. These sets of four answers to the Laws of Media questions complement and connect with each other according to a characteristic common theme. Each set addresses some singular aspect of the Medium's nature, or refers to a particular effect with respect to a small patch of the *ground* against which the Medium's *figure* is cast. Like the structure and predictability offered by poetry's rhyme scheme, the tetrad's four simultaneous and corresponding aspects gives an element of predictability to the multi-faceted nature of any Medium.

Like poetry's rhyme scheme, the tetrad's four corresponding aspects give an element of predictability to the nature of any Medium.

The Tetrads in Motion: Foosball

Let's see how this works by taking an example and working through the tetrad's probes. A common affectation of the dot-com enterprise was the seemingly ubiquitous, and now clichéd, "foosball" table. Foosball is a game played on a rectangular tabletop with raised sides. Rods with several plastic soccer players are installed in these side walls, the plastic players painted one of two colours. Rods of one colour alternate with the other. A ball is launched onto the tabletop and, by turning the rods, the players "kick" the ball, attempting to direct it into one of two goals located at the ends of the table. Each goal, naturally, is defended by one of the two players.

The game has been a standard fixture in bars and pubs for many years and was adopted by the young entrepreneurs of Silicon Valley and elsewhere. Foosball proponents often describe the game as a way of blowing off steam. In other words, foosball is a way to reduce the stress that typically plagues employees working long hours in start-up companies. Clearly, then, it simultaneously OBSOLESCES stress while enabling relaxation. When stress reduction is EXTENDED to the extreme, it may result in losing one's edge or sense of urgency for the task at hand. In this case, too much foosball may become a distraction that could result in lower output or quality.

We now have answers for three of the four Laws of Media questions with respect to the stress-reducing nature of foosball. If we as managers were contemplating the pros and cons of acquiring a foosball table for the lunch or employee recreation room, we would have two factors to consider: The game reduces stress in our employees, but too much time playing foosball may reduce the quality and quantity of work. One could say that these are relatively obvious observations. However, the Laws of Media tell us that there remains one more consideration from the perspective of a competitive, recreational game that reduces stress: "What does foosball RETRIEVE from the past that had been formerly OBSOLESCED?"

One possible RETRIEVAL is the sort of training jousts and man-to-man combat that occurred during the Middle Ages among a king's cadre of knights. These were used to hone fighting skills and improve what we now call the competitive edge of the royal fighters. As we explore this RETRIEVAL aspect through the medieval metaphor, concepts of competition within the ranks, potential development of interpersonal conflicts and animosities, an every-man-for-himself mentality and other heroic attributes come to mind. Interestingly, this psychology seems to translate almost directly to the stereotypical macho and heroic style of software development that often comes from relatively immature software companies today.

Much has been written about the deleterious effects of competitive but solitary programmers being allowed to develop substantial portions of software products alone. Many companies have undertaken initiatives to counteract this mentality among their programmers. However, these efforts may stand in stark opposition to the Message of the foosball table. Unless the company specifically wants to promote the individualistic and aggressive type of behaviour that foosball RETRIEVES, it would seem that the foosball table may reinforce an undesirable psychology among the staff who play the game.

Answers to all four probes must be sought to understand the quality and traits of the Medium and its influence on us.

Without the framework of the tetrad, a company's managers might end their consideration of foosball tables with a generally understood code of behaviour that speaks to managing time and delivering product commitments on schedule. The mental rigour introduced by the tetrad reminds us that all four aspects exist simultaneously: Answers to all four probes must be sought in order to more completely understand the quality and traits of the Medium and its consequences or influence on us. With only a limited, conventional understanding of either the nature of a Medium or its effects, any decisions made will be based on incomplete information — the information we already know, or know about. In this simple example of foosball, using the tetrad allowed us to discover another consideration that was not at all obvious, but whose effect would undoubtedly be felt throughout the organization. We were able to realize that the mentality and behaviour that the game encourages may be contrary to the type of environment and corporate culture that management wishes to create.

In this example we identified characteristics for three conspicuous aspects relating to one theme. The tetrad suggested the existence of the fourth, less evident consideration since three had already been found. More important, we discovered that it was this latent effect that held what might possibly be the more potent Message of the foosball Medium. Potent effects that are not obvious, and perhaps even somewhat obscure are what McLuhan often refers to as a "hidden *ground*." These are the actions of a Medium that we do not consciously perceive, possibly because of the Medium's numbing effects, or because they have receded into the *ground* and are simply ignored. As in the foosball example, it is not the literal image of knights in shining armour that is important, but rather the subsequent transformative thinking that the metaphor stimulates.

The importance of the Laws of Media tetrad framework lies in its ability to reveal characteristics and effects that are hidden. It serves as a flashlight into the dark corners of the mind and shadowed alleyways of perception — areas we may not have visited for quite some time. In the same way that illuminating and searching dark corners at the back of a closet often reveal long-forgotten treasures, so too do the tetrads help recover awareness of effects that are hidden from perception which may prove equally useful and illuminating.

The tetrads even make stating the obvious useful, if not essential. By using obvious characteristics as a starting point in one quadrant, the Laws of Media lead to less obvious realizations via our pursuit of the other aspects. We are forced to think about missing pieces and undiscovered perspectives on the problem or issue — things we haven't yet noticed. More important, deep probing stimulated by the tetrad structure prevents us from either jumping to conclusions or jumping to solutions by forcing us to perceive what we have chosen to ignore: our unconscious assumptions and the unnoticed effects of our environment. An impulse to act without understanding the implications and ramifications of our actions can be checked. We are even encouraged to consider the longer term compound effects — secondary or tertiary consequences that are almost always ignored.

Retrieve Understanding

It is one thing to spot a new product but quite another to observe the invisible new environments generated by the actions of the product. Take Today: The Executive as Dropout, 1972

In the example, the most interesting and revealing exploration came from the RETRIEVES quadrant. This observation seems to be more common than not. As Marshall and Eric McLuhan note, "Retrieval always seems to provide the keynote or dominant mode of each tetrad, which may explain why it is often the most difficult of the four to discover."[1] RETRIEVAL is the source of a manager's understanding of precedents — how an analogous medium acted, and how we reacted before.

For a manager who is considering how the next innovation will affect his or her staff or target market, studying the precedent can be particularly revealing. The RETRIEVES quadrant directly furnishes the lessons and experience of history. For instance, a manager may be concerned about the market acceptance of something totally new and different, but he or she need not worry. The Laws of Media tell us that nothing can be so totally new and different that its potential effects and impact cannot be understood. Each quadrant's probe provides us with an aspect of understanding. Taken together, we can understand not only what the new and different Medium may do via EXTENSION, REVERSAL and OBSOLESCENCE, but also how we reacted to its precursor in the past, via RETRIEVAL.

There is no right or wrong way to complete a tetrad as realizations come to each person in their own order. Consider the Laws of Media as applied to a car. Some initial thoughts come to mind: A car EXTENDS one's ability to travel in private. It could EXTEND status or social standing by virtue of the type or brand of car driven. Many car buffs would note that the car literally RETRIEVES "horse-power" from the past. The environmentalists would point to the car EXTENDING urban sprawl.

As we begin the tetrad, several themes, indicated by the superscript numbers, clearly emerge from these initial random thoughts.

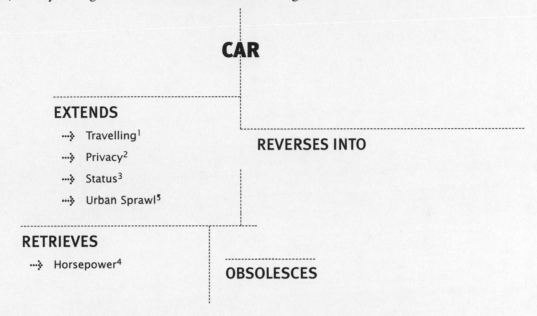

CAR

EXTENDS

···⟩ Travelling[1]

···⟩ Privacy[2]

···⟩ Status[3]

···⟩ Urban Sprawl[5]

REVERSES INTO

RETRIEVES

···⟩ Horsepower[4]

OBSOLESCES

Relative to the *ground* suggested by each of these themes, we ask ourselves the other Laws of Media questions to discover the remaining aspects. For instance, travelling by car obviously OBSOLESCES walking. When car travel is EXTENDED beyond its limits, travel REVERSES into non-travel, that is, the traffic jam. Interestingly, in a traffic jam there is also limited or no privacy, since the drivers of neighbouring stopped cars can afford the distraction of peering through the windows into other cars. If one considers the concept of EXTENDING private travel to large numbers of people at once, another REVERSAL can be identified — private transportation flips into public transportation via buses.

Taking another theme, we observe that urban sprawl, when EXTENDED, REVERSES to create autonomous suburbs, bedroom communities and country living. In doing so, it OBSOLESCES neighbourhoods and a sense of community while RETRIEVING an image of the migrant, the wanderer or the itinerant moving from town to town.

When we think about horsepower, we can easily note that the car OBSO-LESCED beasts of burden by EXTENDING our power, capability and strength to travel faster and to carry heavy or bulky objects. Powerful cars OBSOLESCE the sense of human scale, both with respect to distances and absolute power. However, power REVERSES INTO a lack of energy when "gas guzzlers" over-consume limited fuel reserves. Even greater REVERSALS occur when powerful cars are run to the extreme: They may break down, REVERSING power into impotence; they may be involved in an accident, REVERSING ability into injury, or even death.

The tetrad thus far, with corresponding aspects indicated by the super-scripted numbers, now looks like this:

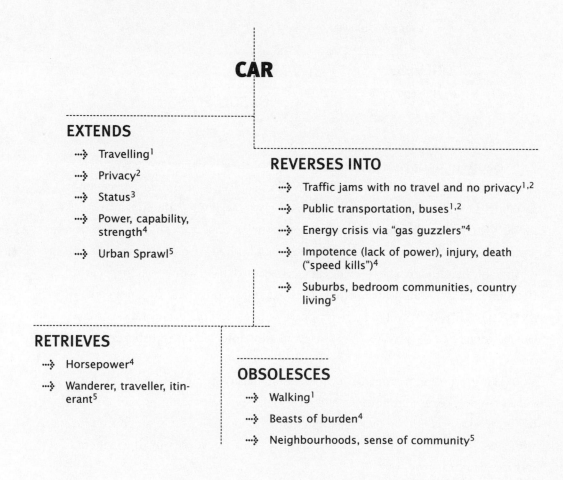

CAR

EXTENDS

- Travelling[1]
- Privacy[2]
- Status[3]
- Power, capability, strength[4]
- Urban Sprawl[5]

REVERSES INTO

- Traffic jams with no travel and no privacy[1,2]
- Public transportation, buses[1,2]
- Energy crisis via "gas guzzlers"[4]
- Impotence (lack of power), injury, death ("speed kills")[4]
- Suburbs, bedroom communities, country living[5]

RETRIEVES

- Horsepower[4]
- Wanderer, traveller, itin-erant[5]

OBSOLESCES

- Walking[1]
- Beasts of burden[4]
- Neighbourhoods, sense of community[5]

From the perspective of automobile marketers, the car EXTENDING status is a key component of many automobile brands. This marketing endeavour is negated by status REVERSING INTO lack of status, or egalitarianism, when everyone can afford a car that purports to be a luxury car — or at least has the toys and trappings of luxury models. It OBSOLESCES humility via an overt display of ostentation and presumed wealth. Luxury models, like the BMW, for instance, became a clichéd status symbol for the up-and-coming MBA graduate when starting salaries permitted large monthly lease payments. Thinking about ostentation and EXTENDING travel, one is reminded of the sedan chair, borne by carriers as the preferred mode of travel for the very wealthy upper class in certain cultures during a long-past era. From the perspective of status, the car RETRIEVES the servant class from the past — in this era, that servant class is made up of mechanics, car washers, gas station and parking lot attendants and other related jobs.

Having asked the Laws of Media questions for each theme, the completed tetrad reveals the following connected aspects:

CAR

EXTENDS

- Travelling[1]
- Privacy[2]
- Status[3]
- Power, capability, strength[4]
- Urban Sprawl[5]

REVERSES INTO

- Traffic jams with no travel and no privacy[1,2]
- Public transportation, buses[1,2]
- Egalitarianism[3]
- Energy crisis via "gas guzzlers"[4]
- Impotence (lack of power), injury, death ("speed kills")[4]
- Suburbs, bedroom communities, country living[5]

RETRIEVES

- Sedan chair[1,2,3]
- Servant class (e.g. mechanics, car washers, gas attendants, etc.) [3]
- Horsepower[4]
- Wanderer, traveller, itinerant[5]

OBSOLESCES

- Walking[1]
- Humility (via ostentation)[3]
- Beasts of burden[4]
- Sense of human scale (distance)[1] and (power)[4]
- Neighbourhoods, sense of community[5]

There are undoubtedly additional themes that can be discovered from thinking about cars and the four Laws of Media probes. Remember that if an answer to one of the questions reveals a new characteristic, answers to the remaining three questions corresponding to the newly revealed characteristic also exist in the other quadrants. As with many quests for knowledge and understanding, it is the most difficult and challenging aspects that are likely to be the most revealing. In some cases, a truly appropriate and insightful characteristic defies discovery for a long time. Nonetheless, we can be assured of its existence: The Laws of Media tetrad tool prompts and encourages its user to search out the hidden, non-obvious shadows of thought from which new insights emerge.

The progress of each theme and the tetrad overall is different for everyone according to the mental and metaphorical connections they make. Here, for instance, an obvious perspective on the car yields an answer in one quadrant. The initial answer to one of the Laws of Media questions leads us to suggestions for another quadrant and on it goes. New themes may occur at any time and in any order. When faced with an unyielding quadrant, we know there is an unanswered question, some aspect of the Medium that we do not yet understand. Nonetheless, through the tool, we at least have the awareness that something is missing. The tetrad helps us realize that an avenue of investigation exists which would otherwise remain hidden from perception — potential consequences completely unexplored and ignored.

> As with many quests for knowledge and understanding, the most difficult and challenging aspects are likely the most revealing.

The specific characteristics in each quadrant are themselves jumping off points for further inquiry. For instance, RETRIEVING the itinerant or wanderer from the past may bring to mind the probe, "What did he need to survive during his journey and find his way from town to town?" Investigating this probe may lead to new product or service ideas pertaining to wayfaring, provisioning or accommodation. Since probing RETRIEVAL often brings back an old cliché as a nostalgia-laden archetype, this quadrant is frequently the source of marketing, advertising and slogan ideas — perhaps in this case, the return of the prodigal son in his late-model, two-door hardtop.

Another example: Reflecting on "Status" in the EXTEND quadrant led us eventually to RETRIEVING the "Servant class" by way of those who maintain and attend to cars. In an era when servants were relatively commonplace — and to some extent it remains true today — good help was hard to find. Since increasing customer satisfaction often leads to loyal repeat buyers, contemplating various types of servants or hired help relative to car quality and longevity may, by analogy, lead to appealing service innovations.

Foretelling the Present

Having characteristics that answer each quadrant's question allows us to look at any particular aspect as *figure* in itself and pose one of McLuhan's most useful probes, namely, "...and what does this change?"[2] This probe invariably leads us down another path of thought, involving other Media upon which the first acts and effects its Message. By examining the changes effected by individual aspects of the Medium's Message — in particular, those aspects that may be obscure at first — a pattern of effects may begin to emerge. These effects help us "foretell the present," since they are, in fact, already acting now.

To illustrate this phenomenon, let us take a previous example as applied to the introduction of a new technology. Recall the analysis of the computer's tetrad that we discussed in the previous chapter. Here is an extract of the four aspects pertaining to one theme:

The future of the future is the present. Take Today: The Executive as Dropout, 1972

COMPUTER

EXTENDS

···❯ Authority of stored information

REVERSES INTO

···❯ "Garbage in, garbage out"

···❯ Over-reliance on one information source to the exclusion of others

RETRIEVES

···❯ Perfection of recall
Total, complete, accurate

OBSOLESCES

···❯ Judgement

In this example, RETRIEVING "Perfection of recall" resulted in the observation that the computer EXTENDED the presumption of "Authority of [computer-] stored information." This, in turn, led to the REVERSAL concept of unquestioning over-reliance on computer-generated information, to the point of OBSOLESCING judgement — trusting the potentially untrustworthy. If managers had this awareness-enabling thinking tool at the time they originally considered the nature and impact of the computer, they could have asked the salient question: "… and what does this change?" The answer would have been instructive.

The Spread of Spreadsheets

Consider the predominance of spreadsheet software and its role in business decisions. Spreadsheet applications were the primary motivators for businesses to first acquire personal computers in large numbers. Spreadsheets are often used to construct quantitative models of a business's operation, most often in a financial context. As with any model, spreadsheet-based models should come reasonably close to accurately describing aspects of real business operations. That is, the model should be able to explain both history and actual current events. Moreover, it should provide some reasonable estimation of future operations that will be close enough to real experience to be useful. However, when spreadsheets — and personal computers — were relatively new, business planners relied on them to mechanically generate forecasts without adequate calibration or verification with the real world.

Because the information came from The Computer, its veracity was unquestioned. Business growth was steady and regular, increasing year-over-year by a fixed percentage, simply because this model was easy to program by novice users. The spreadsheet, in effect, created conditions of an artificial reality within which business managers and leaders had perfect understanding and complete control. This artificially fabricated business context governed budgets, salaries, hiring, layoffs, production, inventory management — it touched every aspect that impinged on the company's fiscal planning and operations. The forecasts became self-fulfilling: Management geared decisions toward meeting the objectives and operating parameters of their model.

When we ask, "…and what does — did — this change?" we can remember that during the years following mass adoption of spreadsheet models, dynamics of general business management changed rapidly. Technological infrastructures were developed to support increasingly complex technology-based models and the operational metrics required to feed them. Businesses became dependent on technology for not merely reporting on their operations, but for defining the rules of their operations. From many perspectives, management of large corporations went through the 1980s as a technocracy — rule and control by the technology and those who run it.

Businesses became dependent on technology for not merely reporting on their operations, but for defining the rules of their operations.

Key business development initiatives were launched and managed according to the capabilities and functions that the technology was able to deliver. Technocrats compiled ironically named "business rules" that were actually the technology rules by which business operations were defined and run. Business operations that could not be adequately expressed in terms of the language of these rules were treated as mere exceptions and ignored, or dealt with arbitrarily in an *ad hoc* fashion. These occurrences were noted by both the business and technology press who, rather than blowing the whistle on the effects of these practices, hailed the rise in influence and power of the Chief Information Officer. The question that remains, however, is whether the thinking encouraged by the tetrads could have led us to anticipate the effects just described. Certainly we have illustrated a slice of management history that happens to correspond to a retrospective application of the Laws of Media and their resultant, consequential thinking. Sceptics may challenge our interpretation of history by asserting that almost any historical recollection can be explained according to an appropriate application of the right perspective to the right model.

To answer the sceptics, we draw attention to McLuhan's assertion that the Laws of Media only describe the effects that are already acting in the Medium being considered, in other words, the dynamic processes it creates.[3] That we react to the Message and subsequently develop corresponding patterns of behaviour cannot help but happen. Our challenge is to notice them happening, and to govern ourselves accordingly as opposed to numbly following an unnoticed impetus. By noticing — being aware of the Medium's Message — the ultimate results are far from inevitable or preordained. In *The Medium is the Massage* — the title being a sharpened probe for what had become his own cliché — McLuhan points out that, "there is absolutely no inevitability as long as there is a willingness to contemplate what is happening."[4]

> **How the Medium is used does not convey its importance. It is what the Medium changes that governs its potency.**

The Laws of Media focus our thinking on the dynamics of active processes that are enhanced or intensified, eliminated, inverted or reincarnated by a Medium. How the Medium is used does not convey its importance. Rather, it is what the Medium changes, what action it causes and what its lasting effects are that govern its potency. Action, effects and dynamics cannot occur in isolation. They are all intimately entwined with the environment — the *ground* — in which the Medium exists.

Palm Reading

In an earlier chapter, we noted the contrast between the now defunct Apple Newton and the very successful Palm personal digital assistant (PDA) — and its siblings and direct descendents manufactured by Handspring, Sony, IBM and others. Both devices, save for differences in size, could be used for the same nominal purposes. The Newton, during its rather short lifetime, enjoyed a wide variety of available applications, with independent and enthusiastic developers finding more uses across an increasing number of industries and functions. A similar wide selection of applications is the hallmark of the Palm-style platform. For both devices, the initial applications used by almost every new user centre around maintaining a calendar, an address book, and a to-do list. Yet, digital organizers, which had been available for many years prior to both the Newton and the Palm, did not enjoy anywhere near the success of the latter or the cachet of either electronic PDA.

For most intents and purposes, the digital assistant devices are technologically equivalent. The difference in their market success can be understood by considering how their respective Messages were treated by their companies.

The Newton was positioned by Apple as an EXTENSION of the notebook, as demonstrated by the emphasis that Apple's marketing staff placed on the device's handwriting interpretation capability.[5] This was in spite of the fact that the actual utility of this feature was far from what the marketing hype made it out to be. We could legitimately probe what were the lasting effects of, and changes enabled by, the portable paper notebook to use as a guide for predicting the analogous effects of its EXTENSION. Similarly, the pre-Palm digital organizer was an EXTENSION of the traditional date book. Examining Laws of Media effects and subsequent changes caused by date-book technology would indicate the potential of the organizer.

On the other hand, the Palm was viewed from its inception as an EXTENSION of the networked computer. The computer-as-Medium effected tremendous changes, not only on business but on all aspects of society and our culture in general. As connectivity and networking allowed computers to become significant agents of change via the Internet, interconnectivity of Palm-style devices via infrared links and later wireless modems followed suit. The significance of changes effected by Palm-style devices is clear when viewed through the magnifying lens of the Laws of Media tetrad. What may also be clear through the REVERSALS and other aspects are subsequent effects on users of these devices. These secondary effects and other less-than-obvious tetrad aspects could point the way to beneficial product evolution, or warn of impending product demise.

Metaphorically Speaking

Although McLuhan admonishes against focusing on how a Medium is used, sometimes its direct and clear-cut use furnishes the first EXTENSION and obvious OBSOLESCENCE that can be identified. From this starting point, it is important to allow one's mind to engage in the type of metaphorical thinking and probing that will lead away from the obvious. Focusing on the obvious is analogous to the image of a "deer caught in the headlights." The deer is frozen in the path of danger, completely unaware of its impending, untimely end because the bright headlights loom so plainly before it. In an analogous way, focusing on the obvious reinforces a state of being unaware of a Medium's true effects. Paradoxically, total focus on what is plainly before us masquerades as complete awareness — but all other thought processes are completely paralyzed.

Paradoxically, total focus on what is plainly before us masquerades as complete awareness. All other thought processes are completely paralyzed.

Think of it this way: When an idea is obvious, we need less thinking to assimilate and understand it. Conversely, when an idea seems difficult, indistinct or ill defined, we require much more brain-power to work it through in order to grasp its essence and meaning. Since thinking — especially critical thinking — is directly tied to awareness, the more obvious something is, the less critically aware of its effects we become, and vice versa.

Language itself — the words we use — can also become so obvious that instead of encouraging thinking, it numbs our mentality and decreases awareness. This realization was the underpinning of our approach to management clichés and cliché-probes. McLuhan realized that language works metaphorically: A particular word conjures up the thought of the actual thing according to the user's frame of reference, or *ground*. Unlike languages based on ideograms like Chinese or Japanese, in a phonetic-based alphabetic language like English, the word itself bears no relationship whatsoever to the thing. It is merely the meaning we have arbitrarily associated with the word that enables the metaphor. As words become obvious, our awareness decreases accordingly. We no longer reach for the richness of meaning conveyed by the metaphor. It takes too much thinking.

For instance, when first introduced to the McLuhan Equation, "the Medium is the Message,"[6] a casual reader will naturally take the common meanings for Medium — a conveyance of information — and Message — the information content. The meaning of McLuhan's paradox is seemingly obvious; the casual reader, however, has gained no additional awareness, insight or perception. To stimulate thought, and thereby new awareness, McLuhan used the terms, Medium and Message, as new metaphors with unconventional meanings. These concepts are not particularly difficult in the context of McLuhan's usage. However, their metaphorical characteristics are nonetheless sufficiently rich to encourage new thinking about even everyday objects that become "Media" through McLuhanesque perception.

Likewise, the Laws of Media tetrads work by encouraging us to use metaphors to kick-start new thought processes. We thereby create a state of heightened awareness by which we can obtain new insights into the nature and effects of a Medium.

But a man's speech should exceed his *gasp*, else what's a metaphor?

Taking the Temperature

As he explored how various Media affected our senses and mental processes, McLuhan noticed that some Media require a higher degree of human sensory participation in their effect, and others a lesser degree. A Medium that provides its content in high definition and is all encompassing, for instance, would require very little mental activity on the part of its user to "fill in the blanks." Such a Medium could easily be an unnoticed environment — all *ground* — and just as easily ignored. On the other hand, some Media are very involving and cannot be ignored, regardless of their content. As we encounter such a low definition Medium — one that provides only limited information — we automatically reach out with multiple senses and a high degree of mental participation to comprehend it. McLuhan characterized these two types as Hot and Cool, respectively.

A Hot Medium is one that requires very little in the way of overall sensory involvement. A Cool Medium requires a high degree of sensory and mental involvement, necessitating active participation by its users.

A Hot Medium is one that requires very little in the way of overall sensory involvement, although one sense in particular is typically emphasized to the exclusion of the rest. On the other hand, a Cool Medium requires a high degree of sensory and mental involvement, necessitating active participation by its users to "complete the picture." These are not difficult concepts in themselves. However, for most people, the specific terminology selected by McLuhan to describe the concepts seems counterintuitive: They are not aligned with our common linguistic metaphors. By now, it is easy to see that this is perfectly consistent with McLuhan's approach to everything — the words themselves are probes into the mind. As he wrote, "To understand media, one must probe everything ... including the words ... and oneself."[7]

McLuhan contended that, as a Medium, speech contains an actual thought process and hence is a direct pathway to mental activity. Had he merely chosen to adopt the common metaphor or definition for Hot or Cool, thinking, awareness and insight would decrease. However, by forcing us to consciously recalibrate our thinking to accommodate his metaphors, our awareness is heightened precisely at the moment we are considering whether a Medium is Hot or Cool. The inconsistency between our conventional usage of the words Hot and Cool, and McLuhan's definitions of Media Temperature are a probing/awareness technique for us to stop and rethink. In doing so, we become acutely aware of our mental dynamics and processes. If the language probe were obvious, then we would be stuck once again in unawareness — the realm of the hidden ground — back to the beginning of attempting to notice.

Television: Cool to Hot

McLuhan experienced the invention of television during his lifetime. When it was new, television was a Cool Medium. It demanded a high degree of multi-sensory involvement, since its magic was naturally engaging while its sensory nature was indistinct. The black and white pictures were of relatively low resolution, and the screen was often awash in static-y, unstable images. Sound quality was not very good, and because many of the programs were obviously on a theatre-like stage set, the audience could naturally and easily perceive the unreality of what was being broadcast. McLuhan saw television as an extension of the sense of touch, not vision, primarily because the mosaic nature of the picture suggested a more tactile characteristic.

> He wrote that all of our senses are simultaneously involved as we interact with television. Such multi-sensory participation – the hallmark of a cool medium – engages us in a way that demands the active involvement of our entire being. Television in McLuhan's time could not simply be background.[8]

Over time, television heated up, and progressively demanded less and less of its viewers while commanding more and more blind attention. Now, with large screens, surround sound and the ultra-high resolution provided by digital transmission and HDTV format, television has become a very Hot Medium indeed. Those who watch a lot of television become immersed in a world whose reality they allow the Medium itself to define. The concept of "couch potato" simply did not exist at television's birth. Simply put, the television watcher no longer needs to "connect the dots" — the Medium attends to the task of completion itself.

Actually, at the time of mosaic television, completing the image was less of a connect-the-dots exercise and more related to pattern recognition — a far more sophisticated activity, requiring considerably more mental and sensory participation. Business managers will often resort to the cliché of "connecting the dots," particularly when they want to reach a quick, relatively obvious conclusion. The phrase RETRIEVES a childhood pastime in which drawing lines from one dot to another completes a picture by following a sequence of numbers along the way. "Connecting the dots" is a very linear activity. In the drawing, the sequence of connection is predetermined to ensure the picture is recognizable upon completion. In business, a linear sequence is necessarily arbitrary — business situations are pictures that are far too complex to be linear. Attempting to impose an *ad hoc* sequence on complexity or the natural chaos of business life will lead to truly insightful conclusions

To understand media, one must probe everything ... including the words ... and oneself.

McLuhan for Beginners, 1997

THROUGH A GLASS DARKLY

Attempting to impose an *ad hoc* sequence on the natural chaos of business life will lead to insightful conclusions only by chance.

only by chance. The chosen outcome would probably be a relatively obvious one from among the many that are possible.

When television was a Cool Medium that engaged its viewers, multi-sensory pattern recognition was required to make sense of it all. As it became a Hot Medium, its "dots" were connected for the audience resulting in a smooth, continuous view of the world according to the network producers' predetermination. In business, those who would encourage "connecting the dots" leading to obvious conclusions are advocating linear thinking that suppresses awareness, acceptance of inevitability and predetermination. Like television, business as a Hot Medium immerses all its participants in a world in which the Medium itself defines the participants' perception. Executives, managers, workers, suppliers and customers are disengaged from discerning reality that multi-sensory perception and objectivity qualifies.

Television: Hot to Cool

Television provides a facinating, if not tragic, metaphor for how a Medium can be made to instantly change its relative temperature. Up until September 11, 2001 at 8:42 a.m. Eastern Time, television was a Hot Medium, having evolved from Cool over a period of thirty years or so. It defined the passive, all-encompassing background realm of couch potatoes who typically "checked their minds at the door" upon entering. The tragedy of two hijacked commercial airliners being deliberately flown into the World Trade Center in New York City, together with the subsequent crash of another into the U.S. Pentagon and the downing of a fourth commercial jet, instantly changed the nature of television-as-Medium. Millions of viewers tuned in to witness the subsequent collapse of huge skyscrapers, becoming unwilling, but actively engaged participants in the unfolding horror.

There was immeasurably more occurring at the sites of the tragedy than could possibly be conveyed via the television screen. As the majority of the civilized world watched in a state of shock and confusion, television's Message REVERSED our involvement from being passive observers immersed in a Hot medium to active participants. We had no choice but to involve ourselves and our senses all-at-once, simultaneously attempting to see more, hear more, smell and feel more. We knew instinctively that television could not possibly portray the magnitude of such an unimaginable and unprecedented tragedy. Our minds tried to fill in the blanks and perform the completion. Television became instantly Cool when we, the audience, were immersed in icy reality.

Ironically, when the trivial was called "Reality TV," television was Hot. Television became Cool again when stark, horrific events were forced upon us, completely banishing the trivial from our collective consciousness.

Television became instantly Cool when we, the audience, were immersed in icy reality.

And what does this change? The most noticeable immediate effect was how television RETRIEVED its mode of programming from the time of its inception. When television was originally Cool and mosaic, the talking news anchor-commentator was the primary content focus. Every network, for most of the first week after the tragedy, reverted to this form. Within two weeks, the money-raising benefit was mounted — a music/variety show, set on what was a televised theatrical stage, seeking to "touch" viewers with sound and sight in order to obtain their participation in fund raising: multi-sensory, active involvement — hallmarks of the Cool Medium.

People who had shunned television, noting with considerable pride that they had not watched television in so many years, hauled out their old sets to watch the developing events. They followed what intelligent commentary and documentary coverage existed on channels that provided it, avoiding those that quickly reverted to trivial, unfounded opinions. Insightful impressions were carried into discussions and correspondence with other like-minded individuals and groups. Television was engaging these people once again, albeit for a short time.

Those who were content with Hot television naturally returned to their old ways once network producers — faced with mounting bills and a lack of advertising dollars — returned to regular programming. American news, arguably serving the war effort, deliberately reheated itself. Almost every television network is designed to be in the Hot Medium business. However, the tragic events and the considerable effect they had on television — instantly, if only briefly, switching it from Hot to Cool — drew out a new, but perhaps small, audience: those who were engaged and attracted to the Cool Medium. One might be tempted to say that it was the events themselves that engaged this audience segment. But the events, together with the accompanying in-depth coverage, were reported in the press and throughout the Internet. Television remained the Cool Medium of choice.

Television producers take note: Perhaps there is business potential in television as Cool Medium — multi-sensory and sophisticated engagement with active participation by the audience. Before stampeding toward the obvious, remember that active participation by the audience does not necessarily translate directly into interactivity with the show. There will eventually be useful convergence of television with the Internet, but it will be more than merely an ongoing chat session into the television studio or playing a game show along with the on-set contestant. Producers appealing to this previously lost audience will have to maintain the perspective of keeping television Cool.

With the advent of digital television transmission via cable and satellite, there has been a concomitant proliferation of highbrow digital channels with more cerebral content. These channels, too, miss the mark. They continue to focus on content as opposed to the Message. Even for an intellectually-targeted channel, such as the *National Geographic* channel, for instance, their programs are designed for, and exist in, a Hot Medium. Remember that a Cool Medium is one that is engaging, perhaps controversial, appeals simultaneously to multiple senses and encourages the users — viewers — to participate, completing the picture. In many respects, *National Geographic* is Hot; *SexTV* is Cool.

> In many respects, *National Geographic* is Hot; *SexTV* is Cool.

Business: Cool or Hot?

There is also an instructive lesson for businesses not directly involved in the television industry. The more a Medium becomes part of the environment or the *ground*, that is, the Hotter it becomes, the more it takes to effect a REVERSAL to Cool. The converse is also true. Some products lose their marketability and brand identity if the target demographic is forced to think too much or actively engage with the product-Medium. However, we have seen throughout business history that products, services and general business dynamics tend to migrate over time from one side of the Media Temperature spectrum to the other. As managers contemplate the relative temperature of their innovations and situations, they must also gauge the current effects of their Media.

The Medium may be causing effects that are contrary to the business's objectives. As we have seen, this behaviour may be related to the intended audience, recipient or market's degree of engagement. For example, a product manager may count on an innovation's ability to disappear into the *ground*, that is, to become very Hot. A business may be counting on its customers to shut down most routes of perception and critical awareness. Another business may depend on active engagement, or re-engagement, of its audience and therefore may need to transform an overheated Medium into a cooler form. There are as many right answers as there are businesses.

Being a Hot Medium is neither good nor bad for business. In some cases, a business is designed to succeed predicated on its Hot characteristics. Coca-Cola, for instance, would not enjoy its market leadership were it not for the Hot nature of its businesses. Multi-level marketing companies rely on being Hot businesses for their intense, high-definition focus on their own recruitment and distribution systems, and encouragement of their recruits' unwavering acceptance. Teen-oriented fashion and accessories are Hot. Haute couture is Cool until it becomes too popular, at which time it REVERSES into Hot.

It is less important for a business to be either Hot or Cool, so long as its leaders understand which temperature is important for the business's survival and growth. A business built on a premise of Cool — seeking highly engaged, mentally and sensorially-active customers — will wither and die if it shifts to Hot. Levi's jeans were Cool when they left the farm, found their way to the city and were the costume of choice for the rebellious 1960s and 1970s. When their brand was subsumed and faded into the *ground* of popular culture, Levi's went from Cool to Hot. Their customers disengaged and the brand went into a tailspin.

It is less important for a business to be either Hot or Cool, so long as its leaders understand which temperature is important for the business's survival and growth.

When a business REVERSES — either in the tetradic sense, the Media Temperature sense or from the perspective of typical business measures — management is forced to swiftly respond. However, the natural migration from Hot to Cool — or Cool to Hot —is typically long. Indeed, unless a precipitous event occurred, a business awakening one morning to the realization that it is no longer Cool is the culmination of a process that took years to complete. The evolution was so slow that management was caught completely unawares. A swift response and turnabout would not necessarily be in the offing.

Using the Laws of Media tetrads as new thinking tools works towards the goal of increasing awareness and promoting creative, insightful thinking. It would therefore be counter-productive to reduce the tetrad to a paint-by-numbers tool. However, it is worthwhile to note that the elements discovered in certain quadrants often correspond to specific business determinants as we have seen among the many examples in this chapter. To illustrate this, we have laid out these influential factors for business decisions in the tetrad format, although the determinants themselves are not specifically aspects of any particular Medium:

BUSINESS DETERMINANTS BY QUADRANT

EXTENDS

···⟩ Benefits from action / commission

···⟩ Features / functions

···⟩ Potential modes of overuse that will change Media Temperature

RETRIEVES

···⟩ Past reactions and business precedents

···⟩ "Dominant mode," possible key to tetrad's business insights

REVERSES INTO

···⟩ Early warnings

···⟩ Modes of failure

···⟩ Evolution, metamorphosis

OBSOLESCES

···⟩ Business justifications

···⟩ Benefits or detriments from cessation / omission

With these suggestions as guides, and our new facility with McLuhan's thinking tools — *figure* and *ground*, probes and probing techniques, the McLuhan Equation, Media Temperature and the Laws of Media themselves — we can now look at a wide variety of applications, both current and, perhaps, for the future.

6. "we shape our tools and thereafter our tools shape us"

Understanding Media, M
Press Edition, 1994

"Our Laws of Media ...

provide a ready means of identifying

the properties of and actions exerted

upon ourselves by our technologies and media ...

They ... form a practical means

of perceiving the action and

effects of ordinary human tools

and services."

—Laws of Media, 1968

One of our key themes is that of perception — particularly perception of the effects that a Medium's action has "upon ourselves." Determining a Medium's effect remains a particularly difficult perception to achieve. In most cases, the Medium's action occurs in a hidden *ground*, effectively camouflaging the effects from our consciousness. However, it is the particular responsibility of a company's marketing department to seek out the effects of its "new Media" — products and services — to determine their marketability, that is, their eventual acceptance and success once they are introduced to the market.

In an interview with *Business Week*, Wharton Business School marketing professor, Leonard M. Lodish, points to the failed Iridium satellite-based, mobile phone system.[1] Although the $5 billion technology provided almost flawless reception anywhere on the planet via its network of sixty-six satellites, few people acquired the bulky phones and used the premium-priced service. As a result, the company filed for bankruptcy in 2000; its assets were sold like those of so many other high-flying TNT companies, returning pennies on invested dollars.

Lodish contends that the company failed to attract sufficient and sustainable revenue because of a simple failing: The price was so high that few potential customers thought the service was worth its cost. Apparently, no market research was done to determine if people would actually use the service, particularly at the asking price. With the possible exception of those in Iridium's marketing department, it seems clear to most that taking some measure of potential market acceptance of a new product is probably a prudent course — especially before spending the equivalent of a small nation's GDP.

Could any reasonable expectations have been set without investing in market research? One could say that the Iridium service was an EXTENSION of the cell phone, arguably an EXTENSION that was taken to the extreme. Let's look at one possible tetrad for the cell phone:

CELL PHONE

EXTENDS

···⟩ Telephone, beyond physical connection[1]

···⟩ Personal mobility, but within a limited geography[2]

···⟩ Independence, by not requiring "sitting by the phone, waiting for a call"[3]

···⟩ Accessibility, availability and expectation thereof[4]

···⟩ Privacy, by having personal calls come to a personal phone[5]

REVERSES INTO

···⟩ Mobility without geographical limitation[2]

···⟩ Always being "on call"[4]

···⟩ Expectation of immediate availability[3]

···⟩ Lack of autonomy, by always being reachable[2,3,4]

···⟩ Lack of privacy by always being contactable and locatable[2,4,3]

···⟩ Private calls become public information[5]

RETRIEVES

···⟩ "Wireless" (original Marconi radio)[1]

···⟩ "Pay" phones (concept of pay-per-call)[1]

···⟩ Personal page or squire[4]

···⟩ Private messages coming to the emperor, often encoded or encrypted[5]

OBSOLESCES

···⟩ Pay phones (the physical phone booth)[1]

···⟩ Solitude, isolation[2,3]

···⟩ "Down time"[4]

···⟩ Eavesdropping on a phone extension[5]

Was price the only issue that caused the downfall of Iridium's business? We know that this satellite system EXTENDS the cell phone, possibly to the point of moving into REVERSAL aspects. We could legitimately ask: What changes would these effects cause in the lives of those using such a service? Imagine the prospective customers and their nature, and then consider whether such people would relinquish autonomy and a measure of control, or accept the imposition of the REVERSAL expectations.

"WE SHAPE OUR TOOLS AND THEREAFTER OUR TOOLS SHAPE US"

Those who purchased the assets of the original Iridium network, including the satellites, for $25 million may well be able to recoup their investment by finding specifically targeted customers. Whether the business will be sustainable in the longer term remains to be seen as users are changed by the EXTENDED cell phone's effects.

Focus on Focus Groups

Lodish apparently marvelled at the fact that, "No one bothered to ask people if they would actually use the product."[2] The common way for businesses to "ask people" is through the use of focus groups. Market research and survey companies will organize facilitated group discussions among people with a particular demographic profile. These discussions are used to gauge the reactions and opinions of potential customers to new product ideas, advertising campaigns, marketing strategies or even issues of the day. In most cases an honorarium in the range of $40 to $100 is paid as compensation to those who participate.

> Quite often, actual market experience differs considerably from the expectations set on the basis of focus group research.

Companies that use focus groups to test consumer response believe that they have accurately sampled the market and use the results as justification for their marketing decisions. Quite often, actual market experience differs considerably from the expectations set on the basis of focus group research. One notable example of this was the Pontiac Aztek, an oddly designed vehicle introduced by General Motors. In appearance, it could be described as the love child of a *ménage à trois* among a minivan, a sedan and a sports utility vehicle in focus groups. Although the automobile manufacturer extensively tested the vehicle, it met with a lukewarm response at the showroom, necessitating hefty purchase incentives.[3] General Motors even went so far as to feature the vehicle as a bonus giveaway to one of the contestants on the popular television show, *Survivor*, in an attempt to attract the attention of its target market.[4] The relationship between the vehicle and a "deserted" tropical paradise on which the cast members were to "survive" various scripted stunt challenges was tenuous at best.

There are numerous reasons why focus groups do not often accomplish their stated objective. Many point to a well-known phenomenon of group dynamics: Within any random group of people, a natural leader always emerges who will, in this case, sway the opinions of most other group members. But even this opinion leader's views are tainted by the artificial nature of the circumstances. The focus group creates a Cool environment. People are asked to imagine shopping or viewing a commercial in their living room or to think about using a new service while sitting around a table with strangers in the presence of microphones, video recorders and a one-way mirror. Often the advertisements to which the participants are asked to respond are crude mock-ups or mere sketches. But even if a television advertisement is complete and "ready for prime time," focus group members still must fill in the rest of their normal television-viewing environment.

Further, focus groups naturally encourage analytic thinking — facilitators ask *why* an individual likes or dislikes some aspect of the focus item, or how it could be improved. Often, group members are asked to choose among several ideas or concepts, again fully engaging the intellect. What is automatic, or even unnoticed, in real life is the object of intense focus in the focus group. Since the facilitator must obtain the opinions of all participants, focus groups often possess an unnaturally inclusive characteristic. Extroverts frequently self-select for participation by seeking recruitment; those introverts who find themselves in a focus group are drawn out to uncomfortably express opinions in front of strangers — regardless of whether they actually believe them.

Advertisements and marketing campaigns, however, typically reside in a Hot habitat. They are most successful when they work on an unconscious level. After all, actually buying something is an emotional experience. Compare this to justifying a purchase, which is somewhat more rational and intellectual. The Cool detachment of the focus group must give way to the Hot real world of television advertising and supermarket store shelves. Focus groups allow market researchers to measure how people would like to think they will behave when exposed to a particular marketing approach — not how they will actually behave and

We have reached a point of data gathering when each stick of chewing gum ... is acutely noted by some computer that translates our least gesture into a new probability curve. Understanding Media, 1964

react. One cannot predict reactions in a Hot environment from observations made in a Cool one.

The example of focus groups provides us an opportunity to compare and contrast the characteristics of Hot and Cool Media:

Hot Medium	Cool Medium
• Extends a single sense in high definition with lots of information	• Engages multiple senses with low definition; less information for each
• Low in active participation; less "filling in" required by the audience	• High participation, engaging intellect; audience must "fill in the blanks"
• Tends to exclude	• Tends to include
• Engenders specialization and fragmentation	• Engenders generalization and consolidation
• Natural reaction is to numb awareness to mitigate the Hot effects	• Natural reaction is to engage awareness and heighten perception
• Often characterized by short, intense experiences	• Often associated with longer-term, sustained experiences
• Tends to capture or hijack attention	• Tends to attract actively aware attention, freely given

The Cool Focus Group

Does anyone get the 'focus game' right? A company that goes by the public name of Television Preview[5] comes close. Understanding the distinction between Hot and Cool measurements, they perform their market research in as close to the Hot environment as they can possibly construct. People are invited to what purports to be an evening of watching and evaluating pilot episodes of proposed new television shows. Two half-hour situation comedies are shown. After each, the

Ads are not meant for conscious consumption. They are intended as subliminal pills for the subconscious. *Understanding Media, 1964*

audience completes a short questionnaire about the program. As an incentive for participating, six "gift packs" of useful household products are raffled, that may include such things as laundry detergent, paper towels, breakfast cereal, juice, plastic wrap and so forth. Prior to each raffle, audience members are asked to select their choices for the gift pack from various categories of items.

Hundreds of people are assembled in a large hotel ballroom for the previews. At the front of the room, multiple television sets provide a close-to-living-room viewing

The Cool detachment of the focus group must give way to the Hot real world of television advertising and supermarket store shelves.

perspective for each participant. A host explains the agenda for the evening: the shows, the questionnaires, the gift selections, the raffles. He also explains that to closely replicate the real in-home viewing experience, the programs will be shown complete with commercials at the appropriate times. And so the Hot television environment is established for several hundred people at a time.

In reality, the programs are pilot episodes for shows that were never purchased by networks, or episodes of series that were never broadcast in the particular region. This minor ruse ensures that there is little likelihood of a participant having actually seen the program. However, the advertisements are all current — and the true subjects of the test. The gift selection process prior to the first raffle establishes a baseline consumer opinion. The subsequent gift selection measures the change in response caused by watching the advertisements as they are cast against the Hot, in-stream ground of the situation comedy. This is the focus group that has harkened to McLuhan's Message: Hot, spontaneous and intellectually numbed buying intentions more accurately reflect the actions of real consumers, as opposed to those of Cool, reasoned, discussion-oriented focus groups.

Aside from three or four staff, invitation mailing costs, and renting the ballroom for an evening, the only additional expenses are the honoraria for several hundred participants — six $40 cheques sent to the lucky winners, "so that [they] may purchase the products of [their] choice at [their] local supermarket."[6]

Market research seems to work best when it captures its subjects in an environment whose Media Temperature closely resembles that of the actual buying or decision-making experience. The effectiveness of advertising in Hot television can best be determined by testing in a Hot "laboratory."

McLuhanistic Soap Wash in Cool; Rinse in Hot

Consider the consumer packaged goods market — laundry soap, toothpaste, breakfast cereal, toilet tissue and the like. The ideal situation for the packaged goods product or brand manager is for the consumer to walk down the supermarket aisle, take the product off the shelf, place it in the shopping cart and move on, away from the competitors' products. To be successful for the long term, packaged goods must be Hot Media. If the consumer were engaged and thinking critically, there would be the moment's hesitation as competing products are noticed. Comparisons would be made on price, packaging, aroma, longevity, ease of use and other criteria, both objective and subjective. There is a significant chance that a competitor's product would end up in the shopping cart.

Compare the established brand as Hot Medium with the requirements for introducing a new brand to the store shelves. In this case, the brand manager must create awareness in the minds of targeted consumers in order to break the unthinking pattern of grab-place-leave that the incumbent product enjoys. Many well-established techniques are traditionally used, all with the aim of initiating the new brand as a Cool Medium. Advertising is used to capture awareness. Free samples are delivered door to door to engage other senses not easily reachable by advertising — typically taste, smell or touch. So engaged, the consumer is now more likely to try the new product, breaking the old pattern.

At this point, the brand manager must quickly and successfully change the nature of the new product from Cool to Hot so that the new patterns are locked in and become automatic. A continually engaged consumer leaves an open door for the competition to recapture his or her interest. Again, this is often accomplished with an inundation of advertising that overloads one sense to the exclusion of others, thereby

... Ads push the principle of noise all the way to ... persuasion ... quite in accord with the procedures of brain-washing. Understanding Media, 1964

causing a REVERSAL from Cool to Hot. Selecting the new product becomes an automatic part of the consumer's shopping *ground*.

Most Media do not enjoy such aggressive and deliberate management to change their Media Temperatures. Most will evolve by virtue of the changes they effect on their users and environment. When we create a new Medium, it possesses its own sets of effects, some of which are specifically a result of its temperature. These effects change us, our behaviours and reactions. In turn, the ways in which we change either cause us to change the Medium, or to invent yet a new Medium that OBSOLESCES its predecessor. Once a Medium's temperature has been changed, it requires acute, intense awareness on the part of its users to REVERSE it again, allowing it to continue its work with the same temperature effects as before. Otherwise, the cycle of OBSOLESCENCE and subsequent RETRIEVAL is needed for it to once more carry a potent Message.

> A continually engaged consumer leaves an open door for the competition to recapture his or her interest.

The Internet as *Ground*

A recent Medium with a compelling Message is the Internet. Indeed, it would be tempting to perform a McLuhanesque analysis on the Messages of the Internet had Marshall McLuhan not already done so nearly thirty years ago. Of course, he did not call it "The Internet" at the time. Nonetheless, his various analyses of the effects of instantaneous, multi-directional, electronic communications existing everywhere, all-at-once have been remarkably accurate.

Unfortunately, most of these, while interesting, have been of limited practical use for business. The business world's Internet focus has been on the technology or technological-enabling aspects of the Internet, in other words, how the Internet is used. McLuhan, however, reminds us that this is an easily deceptive view. "Our conventional response to all media, namely that it is how they are used that counts, is the numb stance of the technological idiot."[7] Even examining the Internet as *figure* to understand its potential effects is not useful for most businesses unless they are specifically and actually in the "Internet business." Rather, the Internet should be considered as *ground* — perhaps one of several — against which Internet-enabled business endeavours are cast.

Want to Go Shopping? *Cool!*

> **Among the most difficult things to accomplish in business is to change ingrained, highly socialized, established patterns of human behaviour.**

Take online grocery shopping, for example. In the previous chapter, we touched on how the business model for online shopping was ill conceived in many instances. Let's look at Internet-based grocery shopping from the perspectives of the Laws of Media and Media Temperature. It is important to realize that among the most difficult things to accomplish in business is to change ingrained, highly socialized or historically established patterns of human behaviour. As we consider online grocery shopping, bear in mind that we will be casting it as figure against the dual grounds of the Internet and its Media temperature, and deep-seated human social behaviour.

A simple tetrad reveals the following:

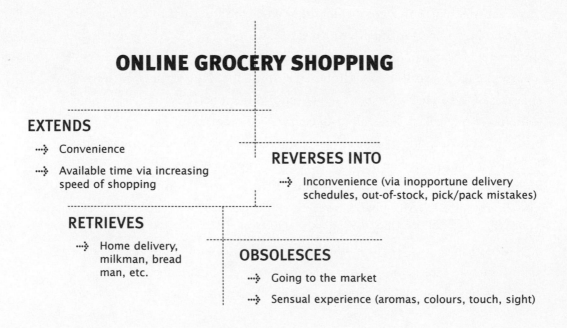

ONLINE GROCERY SHOPPING

EXTENDS

···⟩ Convenience

···⟩ Available time via increasing speed of shopping

REVERSES INTO

···⟩ Inconvenience (via inopportune delivery schedules, out-of-stock, pick/pack mistakes)

RETRIEVES

···⟩ Home delivery, milkman, bread man, etc.

OBSOLESCES

···⟩ Going to the market

···⟩ Sensual experience (aromas, colours, touch, sight)

Noting that online grocery shopping OBSOLESCES "going to the market," what immediately comes to mind is the OBSOLESCENCE of a human behaviour that has existed for thousands of years. The market has traditionally been a place of meeting throughout all of human history, pervading every social culture. In fact, even in modern, western societies, the connection between market and meeting is so strong that in the 1980s, some grocery stores went so far as to explicitly reserve certain evenings at their market strictly as singles' meeting nights.

The other early warning for the online grocer is the OBSOLESCENCE of the "sensual experience" of grocery shopping. For most people, shopping for food is programmed as a sensual experience. Fresh produce and perishables are purchased by most consumers using four of the five senses: Is the produce free of blemishes? Do the seeds rattle freely in the ripe cantaloupe? Are the pears firm or mushy? Is the fish fresh? The only sure way to tell is by smell. Free samples given away in store aisles engage the last sense, that of taste. Supermarkets have introduced in-store bakeries, not only to provide stock for their shelves, but to permeate the store with the aroma of freshly baked bread. Online grocery shopping attempts to circumvent a fundamental human behaviour: On the Internet, shopping for groceries disconnects the sensual via the computer screen avatar.

Shopping is a Cool experience — multiple senses are simultaneously engaged. There is interaction with other people in the market. The sensual involvement naturally leads the shopper to "fill in" the cooking process in the store so that a complete meal can be vicariously prepared and tasted on the mind's tongue from among the ingredients. Online grocery sites attempt to make food shopping a Hot experience — only sight is used; all other senses are shut down. And even the sense of sight is tightly controlled by the shopping site's programmers and graphics designers. Of necessity, convenience and speed offered as beneficial EXTENSIONS diminish engagement and involvement. So not only is online grocery shopping attempting to change basic patterns of behaviour, it attempts to instantly change the Media Temperature of the activity.

In Canada, GroceryGateway.com is the main entrant into the online grocery business. Their advertising primarily centres on images of the grocery deliveryman, rendered in a graphic reminiscent of 1950s

Food for the mind is like food for the body: The inputs are never the same as the outputs.

Take Today: The Executive as Dropout, 1972

"WE SHAPE OUR TOOLS AND THEREAFTER OUR TOOLS SHAPE US"

> **Not only does online grocery shopping attempt to change patterns of behaviour, it also attempts to instantly change the Media Temperature.**

and 1960s style artwork, dressed in a uniform that is also in the style of that time. This clearly draws from the RETRIEVAL quadrant, an attempt to capitalize on positive nostalgia associated with home delivery of milk, bread and groceries in the minds of people who were then children.

What is also interesting is that some of the company's early problems — and they certainly were not alone among online grocery sites in this regard — had to do with the REVERSAL items: Scheduling convenient delivery times with customers and incorrect or missed items.

Although online grocery shopping was a much lauded application that could only exist by virtue of the Internet, none of the foregoing discussion focuses on the technology of the Internet or the specific attributes of the Internet. They are simply not relevant to understanding the nature and effects of online grocery shopping. How the Medium of the Internet is used is not an important consideration for understanding its effects as a *ground* for business.

The demise of the major U.S. entrants in this business may well have been predictable via a simple understanding of the nature and effects of online grocery shopping as a Medium. To be fair, this is not to say that there will never be a market segment that would buy from an online grocer. What this analysis does is provide a clear warning as to what the behavioural challenges would be and how a large market would likely react. Despite being faced with the warning, any clever entrepreneur is welcome to invest time and money to attract a well-targeted segment that will sustain his or her business. Such a selective customer segment may not necessarily be as prone to the identified Laws of Media effects because of their unique *ground*.

There is danger in ignoring what the OBSOLESCENCE quadrant reveals if what is being OBSOLESCED is fundamental to human nature or behaviour. Another clear warning for business often lurks among the effects in the REVERSAL quadrant. In most corporations, sponsors or promoters of a particular initiative often become so enamoured with their innovation that they tend to carry it to the extreme. In Chapter 3, we noted how the typical adversarial environment characteristic of many corporate cultures may demand this level of unwavering loyalty in order to ensure the survival of one's idea. For example, those who have had formal education in brand management know that brand extension is a traditionally accepted method for sustaining the popularity, market share and revenue associated with a particular product. There seems to be a primary business imperative that favours EXTENSION and enhancement. As such, there is an ever-increasing risk that for a given Medium — product, service, brand or idea — REVERSAL effects will become evident and eventually displace EXTENSION as the predominant Message.

The REVERSAL of Television
We Now Pause for a *Message* from
Our Sponsor

Relative to the *ground* of North American culture, television REVERSED its Media Temperature, from being a Cool Medium at its inception to a Hot Medium now, over a span of about thirty years. The Internet appeared on the horizon of the general public's consciousness late in 1993 with the invention of the World Wide Web and the Mosaic browser. It was a Cool Medium. Within a few years, the Internet became Hotter and, as a Medium, receded into *ground*. It became the environment, setting the context for other business discussions. Almost every business of significant size challenged their CIOs to develop an "Internet Strategy," in effect saying, "I don't care what goes on the Web, so long as we *are* on the Web." To senior management, Internet presence alone was the issue, much to the consternation of the technologists who believed that management did not "get" the Internet. They actually "got" it quite fine — content did not matter because the Medium is the Message. In other words, simply having the Internet as a context would result in effects to which the business would respond. Management felt that these effects would help set the future agenda for new business initiatives and changes.

The Internet as context would result in effects that would help set the future agenda for new business initiatives.

Business managers, and particularly those who were involved with failed Internet-based endeavours, now lament how the unwillingness of the audience to pay for content precludes a viable online business. Anthony B. Perkins, editor-in-chief of *Red Herring* magazine, wrote "No industry segment was more devastated during the

Internet company shakeout than the so-called Web media space. ... My personal analysis is that there was never a viable business model for a single media brand to build any kind of significant Web franchise, never mind make money at it."[8]

Web media content companies, like Yahoo, for example, charge content producers to distribute their material. This clearly RETRIEVES the relationship between television networks and television producers. When television was new, networks primarily produced their own content and developed their own stars, RETRIEVING the earlier Hollywood studio model. Later, as television matured, the production shifted in favour of independent production companies. Independent producers dominated the development of programming, selling their products to networks that had adopted the role of content distribution companies. The networks' own production eventually became limited to news and "news magazine" format programs. As mere intermediary distribution channels, the number of networks proliferated: Now, the traditional broadcast networks are merely a few among hundreds of cable and digital networks.

Television evolved from a Cool Medium to a Hot one. Over the same period, the television business model similarly evolved. Initially, advertisers paid for production and distribution more or less directly, as the networks themselves played both roles. Next, advertisers paid the networks for the particular distribution of specific programs; the networks, in turn, paid the program producers. The viewer still was able to watch for free, aside from the initial cost of the television set. With the advent of a better physical distribution capability — cable — viewers were asked to pay for the improved distribution. Improving the quality and definition of the reception contributed to television heating up, as less was being demanded of the viewers to complete the picture.

As the evolution continued, distribution companies — now including satellite — assumed a role more akin to content aggregators as well as distributors. In this role, the cable and satellite companies collected content fees from the viewers and disseminated them proportionally to the networks and from there to the content producers, keeping a fee for themselves in providing this intermediary service. Users willingly paid for unique or specialized programming that was not available through the free broadcasters, and for the privilege of reduced or no commercial advertising.

What actually happened? Television was initially a Cool Medium. Its users — the viewers — did not pay to use the Medium or receive the content. Content production and distribution was funded by sponsors who were interested in reaching an engaged audience. There were essentially no intermediaries in the path of the Medium. As television heated up — continually EXTENDING and enhancing, to the point of becoming a very Hot Medium — the number of parties involved in the path from content producers to consumers increased. In particular, this included the addition of pure intermediaries who did nothing but collect a fee for being part of the distribution mechanism. Users willingly paid for the privilege of continuing their complete immersion in an all-encompassing *ground*.

As we consider Web media companies on the Internet, all of this reasoning is central to its RETRIEVAL quadrant, which provides the keynote or "dominant mode." Let's begin the tetrad at RETRIEVES, and fill in the rest:

Users willingly paid for the privilege of continuing their complete Immersion in an all-encompassing ground.

WEB MEDIA CONTENT COMPANY (FINANCIAL ASPECTS)

EXTENDS
⋯⋗ Availability of unique or specialized value, hence increased likelihood of payment, *Note: the greater the extension, the Hotter the Medium becomes*

REVERSES INTO
⋯⋗ Non-unique value (ubiquitous availability of similar content), hence unwillingness to pay

RETRIEVES
⋯⋗ TV Network / Producer model

OBSOLESCES
⋯⋗ Free content
⋯⋗ Cool-ness

One clear observation, easily confirmed by everyday experience, is that people will generally pay for what they perceive to be unique value. For producers, offering that value is not necessarily easy, particularly when similar content is readily available from many sources. The RETRIEVAL also suggests that as the Medium heats up, there is increased opportunity for intermediaries to find useful positions among the effects of the Medium. In its earliest days, some observers enthusiastically predicted that the Internet would cause "disintermediation," that is, the elimination of middlemen from business transactions. It is now clear that this perception applied primarily while the Internet was relatively Cool. As it heated up, new intermediaries found places analogous to those that existed in pre-Internet business relationships.

One need only think of payment transfer agents, dispute resolution mediators, online advertising agencies, a multitude of new-style travel agencies, non-participatory trade exchanges, employment agencies and many other similar businesses. Some may say that none of these businesses is really necessary given the Internet's ability to enable direct communication among the principals of a business interaction. While this may be technologically true, those who subscribe to this view regard the Internet as a Cool *figure* relative to a non-networked business *ground*. However, this does not correspond to the Internet's current Media Temperature. It has become a Hot *ground*, and as such, will allow intermediaries to flourish.

This analysis suggests one last probe, and we offer it as an exercise to find additional examples. We have left it as a probe for several reasons: First, there is often more value in the process of discovery that a probe encourages than in the answer itself. Second, the probe's suggestion may not necessarily hold true in every case, and we certainly do not want to encourage business managers to jump to conclusions. Nonetheless, it seems valid when applied to the business models associated with many diverse Media. The probe: Are users more willing to pay for using a Hot Medium than a Cool one? Like television, the Internet has become Hot. If the probe is answered in the affirmative, the time may be ripe to OBSOLESCE the online advertising model as a

It is not possession of the solution, but the recognition of the problem itself that provides a resource and the answers.

Take Today: The Executive as Dropout, 1972

source of revenue for Web media content companies — although declining revenue suggests that it may already have been OBSOLESCED — and drag users to a pay-for-valuable-use business model in one way or another.

Jobs, Roles and Other Pastimes

The Laws of Media "apply to all human artefacts, whether hardware or software, whether bulldozers or buttons, or poetic styles or philosophical systems."[9] We have so far focused on products, services and other more or less tangible aspects of business. However, the Laws of Media apply equally, and are equally useful, to considerations of more abstract concepts of business management. In fact, during our earliest forays into applying these thinking tools to complex business problems, one of the first tetrads we constructed probed the effects of working excessive hours and the problem of employee burnout:

WORKING EXCESSIVE HOURS

EXTENDS

- ···⟩ Working hours (Time spent)
- ···⟩ Number of commitments
- ···⟩ Personal expectations
- ···⟩ Accomplishments
- ···⟩ Comfort Zone

REVERSES INTO

- ···⟩ Burnout
- ···⟩ Frustration, disappointment
- ···⟩ Anger
- ···⟩ Non-productivity (Time wasted)

RETRIEVES

- ···⟩ Hunter (must constantly hunt or can't eat)
- ···⟩ Slavery
- ···⟩ Short life span (Time limited)
- ···⟩ Industrial revolution, Assembly line
- ···⟩ Specialist/ism

OBSOLESCES

- ···⟩ Satisfaction, Pride of Accomplishment
- ···⟩ Happiness
- ···⟩ Sense of ownership
- ···⟩ Productivity
- ···⟩ Personal Time
- ···⟩ Relationships

"WE SHAPE OUR TOOLS AND THEREAFTER OUR TOOLS SHAPE US"

It is interesting and seemingly paradoxical that Working Excessive Hours, a hallmark of the modern economy, RETRIEVES such mechanistic and archaic concepts as the Industrial Age factory assembly line. Jobs mean specialization and fragmentation of tasks in a manner that is well suited to the industrial model. In factories, for example, a larger task is broken down into a set of the smallest possible tasks for particular individuals to perform with automaton-like repetition. Fragmentation meant that the context of the larger task was lost on individual workers. Pride of accomplishment and a sense of ownership were OBSOLESCED. And what did that change? Individual accountability was eliminated and overall quality diminished.

The industrial model was carried over from blue-collar workers to non-factory employees. Many, if not all, of the negative behaviours and symptoms exhibited by assembly-line workers were also manifest in white-collar, burned-out, job-oriented employees. Considering that jobs are extensions of our highly specialized hands, it seems that often relatively little involvement is needed beyond the literal "task at hand." Jobs are a Hot Medium.

Conversely, roles mean generalization and flexibility. An individual in a role is required to use a variety of skills and experience, applying them to various situations. Being in role suggests drawing on attributes and characteristics, rather than merely demonstrating a specific skill. A role necessitates the ability to assume a character or persona appropriate to the situation, much like the actor does on stage. In doing so, the individual must consolidate a relatively large amount of information and respond in a manner more akin to pattern recognition than mechanistic "connecting the dots." There is total and active involvement of multiple senses, as the person-in-role continuously monitors, adjusts and responds to a dynamic, and often unpredictable, environment. Roles are a Cool Medium.

The "Specialist," RETRIEVED in this tetrad, is considered a highly valued individual — so highly valued in fact that many companies will extend special privileges to keep their specialists satisfied and on the job. However, the concept of "Specialist" as the source of knowledge or particular experience is quite contrary to McLuhan's view of roles

In the computer age we are once more totally involved in our roles. Understanding Media, 1964

replacing jobs. He writes, "With automation, it is not only jobs that disappear, and complex roles that reappear. Centuries of specialist stress in … the arrangement of data now end with the instantaneous retrieval of information…"[10]

One could legitimately assert the value of specialists. After all, someone must have the depth of technical knowledge required to design routing networks for telecommunications companies. Rocket scientists and brain surgeons will always be needed. It seems obvious that deep technical knowledge will continue to be necessary in one field or another.

The specialist as "container of knowledge" — job — must give way to the person who is an applier of expertise — role.

Deep technical knowledge without the ability to apply it to new situations, however, has limited value, and can certainly be replaced by electronic devices and networked computers. This contention is fundamental to McLuhan's declaration that the age of specialists has passed with the instantaneous availability of information. The specialist as "container of knowledge" — job — must give way to the person with knowledge who is an applier of expertise — role. If it is merely the depth of knowledge for which an individual is valued, then that individual serves only as a convenience, saving the relative layperson from the trouble of personally obtaining the information electronically.

We have already seen an analogous revolution in the patient-doctor relationship. A knowledgeable patient, armed with information from credible medical Web sites, engages his or her physician in active consultation about options in his or her course of treatment. For the physician who regarded him- or herself as the source of wisdom and knowledge, this has been a threatening, and in some cases, traumatizing, transition. However, for the physician used to assuming multiple roles of teacher, mentor, advisor as well as skilled practitioner, the knowledgeable patient is a godsend. Both doctor and patient are fully engaged; medical outcomes are improved and the patient has a greater sense of control over his or her own destiny. This is very Cool.

In a corporate setting, consider the person with a considerable depth of knowledge placed in a variety of roles, as opposed to being kept tightly contained in the lab, the marketing department or some other job. Place that knowledgeable individual in areas as diverse as sales, strategy, or finance in the role of teacher, storyteller, visionary, leader or builder. That role-player can now offer tremendous value to the corporation by virtue of the changes he or she can effect. Remember — the power and value of a Medium is measured not in its use, but rather in the nature of the changes it can bring about.

Companies squander the value of their people if they are kept in jobs. How often do highly qualified, motivated people with considerable corporate seniority hear the refrain of, "You're too valuable in your job to transfer somewhere else. Keep doing what you're doing." At times of high job mobility, a motivated individual will simply walk out the door to find the appropriate opportunities. On the other hand, companies that view their personnel from the perspective of roles will naturally have an advantage over those that do not. Role-oriented managers are able to capitalize on the creative and original thinking that is naturally introduced into any process when a person with a depth of knowledge in a different functional area is allowed to bring a new context to an old problem.

Hot jobs versus Cool roles influence hiring dynamics as well. When hiring, the person with the most experience and qualifications may not be the one best suited for the position overall. A person brought into a new role should be sufficiently challenged so as to be EXTENDING him- or herself to fill the requirements of the role. Hiring to the role requires a candidate to possess more than the technical qualifications to be able to perform. It also necessitates many attributes and the appropriate attitude associated with an ability to learn and assimilate the lessons of new experiences. What a hiring manager should be looking for is the Message of a new hire — the effects that can be introduced — and less of the specific content. Contrast this with the person brought into a job whose key attribute is extensive experience — so extensive that he or she has EXTENDED his or her ability or willingness to assimilate new experiences beyond the reasonable limit. Inevitably, this person REVERSES into the problem employee, often characterized by a bad attitude.

A person hired into a job will often end their day exclaiming, "I hate my job." But, "I hate my job" cannot translate to "I hate my role," since roles are a put-on — they are assumed — and can be taken off and changed as situations change. Roles are a way in which people define

The primitive hunter or fisherman did no work .... Where the whole man is involved there is no work. *Understanding Media, 1964*

their identity within a context, since they are self-realized. Jobs, on the other hand, are imposed by the company and can easily be hated as an arbitrary identity imposed by an outside agent. The transition of jobs to roles that McLuhan identifies EXTENDS our individual identities. What does it RETRIEVE from the past? John the blacksmith, George the baker, Sam the fishmonger: the pre-industrial sense of role as identity and self-determination. It certainly OBSOLESCES job apathy, disengagement and a "know it all, been there, done that" attitude.

When Media Collide

No medium acts in a vacuum. McLuhan says, "No medium has its meaning or existence alone, but only in constant interplay with other media."[11] While this may be abundantly clear when one considers tangible Media — a car interacting with a road, for instance — it is less clear what the effects may be when concepts-as-Media interact. In business, however, the most astronomical problems tend to occur when concepts collide. The Laws of Media tetrads offer a useful device to make sense of the resulting cataclysm of ideas, and will often reduce religious debates over whose opinion holds more validity to a compare and contrast discussion.

Multiple tetrads may share one or more concepts in the same quadrant. The REVERSAL quadrant for two or more Media may contain similar characteristics, for example. Or, two separate Media under consideration may both RETRIEVE the same previously OBSOLESCED form from the past. Commonalities in the same quadrant characterize clustered tetrads — where a group of tetrads have at least one, and perhaps several, of the Laws of Media in common. Similarly, multiple tetrads may be chained. Chained tetrads occur when a probe in one tetrad provides the subject Medium, or a different quadrant, of another tetrad.[12]

In business, however, the most astronomical problems tend to occur when concepts collide.

By watching for clusters or chains of tetrads, we can easily detect correspondences, alignments, mutual support and even a measure of effectivity among different Media, be they tangible products, intangible concepts or a mixture of both. Additionally, inconsistencies become immediately clear when

By watching for clusters or chains of tetrads, we can detect correspondences, alignments, mutual support and effectivity among different media.

one Medium's tetrad RETRIEVES what is an OBSOLESCED or REVERSAL item in another. Let's look at an example.

At one time, the issue of Web site "stickiness" was hotly debated among Web portal and online consumer-oriented, retail shopping sites. The term, "stickiness" refers to the amount of time a visitor to the Web site spends browsing its pages or participating in various interactive activities. The question for online retailers was, "Does Web site stickiness increase online Web shopping?" The theory, which was promoted by stickiness supporters, was that the more time a visitor spent at the site, the more likely he would be to buy one of the products. Tens, if not hundreds of millions, of dollars were spent in aggregate by Web retailers in an effort to increase the "stickiness quotient" of their online properties — all based on conjecture and assumptions about the value of stickiness.

This problem was another of the early investigations into using the Laws of Media tetrads to understand the effects of two Media — in this case concept Media — interacting with one another. Here are our original, early tetrads for both Web Site Stickiness and Web Site Shopping:

WEB SITE STICKINESS

EXTENDS

- Visit time at Web site
- Access to "content"
- (Sense of) Community
- Familiarity
- Comfort ("like an old shoe," or "where everyone knows your name")
- Addiction, obsession
- Small world, neighbourhood, locale
- Frequency of visits

REVERSES INTO

- Closed community
- Frustration, feeling of entrapment (can't get out)
- Boredom (same ol' same ol')
- (familiarity breeds) Contempt
- Isolation (from the larger world)
- Apathy
- Provincial attitudes, small town mentality
- "Us" versus "Them"
- Captured audience

RETRIEVES

- Closed/gated community, small town
- Tribe
- Maze
- Muzak (in-house canned programming)
- Mall

OBSOLESCES

- Newness, discovery
- Getting attention
- Portal (to somewhere else)
- External hyperlinks
- Global view, sense of "out there"

"WE SHAPE OUR TOOLS AND THEREAFTER OUR TOOLS SHAPE US"

CONSUMER-ORIENTED WEB SITE SHOPPING

EXTENDS

...⟩ Ability to buy easily ("just enough" time to facilitate the purchase transaction)

...⟩ Physical presence

...⟩ Productive time

...⟩ Comparison shopping (competition is just a click away)

...⟩ Ability to find hard-to-find goods

...⟩ Shopping as need fulfillment

REVERSES INTO

...⟩ Temptation/Ability to browse and become distracted (more than "just enough" time spent, because of too much information, too many choices, too much distraction, too much "content")

...⟩ Detachment, isolation from reality

...⟩ Wasted, non-productive time

...⟩ Price obsession, dissatisfaction, "buyer's regret"

...⟩ Shopping as recreation

...⟩ Shopping as competitive sport ("Look what I found; look what I paid")

RETRIEVES

...⟩ Mail-order, catalogue shopping

...⟩ Home delivery (e.g., milkman, bread man, "the ice man cometh," etc.)

...⟩ Garage sales (especially in the context of online auctions)

...⟩ Hunter-gatherer

...⟩ Personal service (i.e., tailored, customized shopping sites)

OBSOLESCES

...⟩ Public market

...⟩ Shopping as a social activity

...⟩ Personal service (i.e., served by a person)

...⟩ Time taken for other (preferred) activities

From the perspective of Web Site Shopping, time usage is a key factor. Particularly when the items that the consumer is seeking are not especially sensual in nature — technical books and manuals, CDs or software, for example — the convenience of ordering the commodity from an online catalogue provides considerable benefits. When "just enough time" is spent to select and order the desired items, productive time is EXTENDED through the site facilitating a positive shopping experience. However, when the "just enough time" is EXTENDED beyond a reasonable tolerance limit, the experience will REVERSE into some very negative aspects, such as distraction, detachment, isolation, wasted non-productive time and dissatisfaction. Whether the REVERSAL occurs due to a poorly designed interface, a difficult checkout process or other distractions is largely irrelevant.

As it turns out, Web Site Stickiness attempts to increase the time spent at the site by providing as much content as possible, seemingly the antithesis of positive Web Site Shopping attributes. Anecdotal evidence suggests that many content-rich shopping sites have become, in the minds of many potential customers, merely that — Web media content sites. Amazon.com, a major online book retailer that offers free access to book reviews and critiques, may well discover that its virtual browsers outnumber its actual buyers in a ratio that exceeds that of physical storefront booksellers. Or, perhaps book buying is more of a sensual, Cool experience than was originally understood. Witness the evolution of bookstores with the addition of cafés, comfortable chairs, variable lighting and music.

It is interesting to note that many of the REVERSAL aspects of both tetrads are common, possibly indicating that "too much of a good thing" may work against both Web Site Shopping and Web Site Stickiness. In any event, the simple answer to what was a Hot, expensive debate seems to be that consumers who choose to shop online want convenience and speed, not entertainment and distraction. As is so often the case, what becomes apparent through awareness and insight is not necessarily what was originally thought to be obvious.

In retrospect, all great discoveries are obvious. From Cliché to Archetype, 1970

7. busi

"When the trend is one way ... resistance insures a greater speed of change. Control over change would seem to consist in moving not with it but ahead of it.

hot and

ness

Anticipation gives the power to deflect and control force."

—Understanding Media, 1964

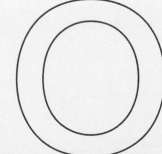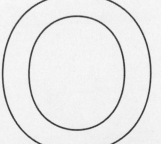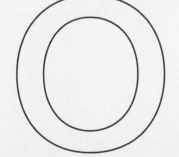

cool

Should a business in a Hot industry itself be a Hot business? Conventional wisdom holds that a business should focus on what it does best. Each of its segments should be managed in "high definition," with as much information as possibly available to guide management's decisions and enable effective business processes. These are generally accepted core principles for doing business in the information-rich "digital economy." Indeed, such special- ization and high definition are characteristic of a Hot Medium. Further, there has been a shift in recent years towards increasing electronic inter-business transactions, and recurring talk about avatars and intelligent agents automatically concluding deals in a virtual exchange or electronic marketplace. These changes are all Hot, encouraging lower human participation, fragmentation of relationships and exclusion.

Managers, enam- oured with a singular *vision* of a business model, often succumb to the numbing effects of the Hot conception of their business.

Recall, however, that the effect of a Hot Medium is to numb awareness and hyper-emphasize a single sense. Managers, enam- oured with a singular *vision* of a business model and its associated tactics, often succumb to the numbing effects of the Hot concep- tion of their business. They often remain unaware of aspects of reality that do not neatly fit within their narrowed view and are not measured by their Hot metrics. In short, they cannot tear themselves away from the object of their intense focus.

In *Understanding Media*, Marshall McLuhan uses the Greek myth of Narcissus as a metaphor for this effect. In the mythological tale, the gods punish the mortal Narcissus for spurning the nymph, Echo. One day, while Narcissus was leaning over the limpid waters of a fountain, he caught sight of his own reflection in the water. Believing the reflection to be a spirit of the fountain, he fell madly in love with the image and, unable to tear himself away from it, died of languor.[1]

McLuhan points out that the name, Narcissus, is derived from the Greek word, *narcosis*, meaning numbness. Contrary to the popular belief that holds that Narcissus fell in love with himself, he actually met his tragic fate by being caught up by the Hot image of reality. He could not recognize the reflection for what it was; his extreme focus using only one sense resulted in numbing all other perceptions.

Recently, many managers whose businesses collapsed in the meltdown of new, Internet-based or dependent dot-com companies were accused of hubris. While this label is clearly justified for some, for others, it may be unfair. Rather, they may simply have succumbed to McLuhanesque Narcissism, that is, being obsessively focused on one aspect or objective of their business to the exclusion of any other considerations. In other words, they were Hot managers of Hot businesses.

Exodus Communications

The story of Ellen Hancock, the former CEO of Exodus Communications, may be an illustrative, if not cautionary, tale. Exodus once led the market for co-location facilities — managed datacentres in which companies would house their computer and network operations. Exodus provided secure rack space in which computers were physically located, reliable electrical power, air conditioning and telecommunications, as well as various degrees of operational monitoring, depending on the service level chosen by the customer. Each client installation was housed in either a separate or shared locked cage.

According to a statement issued by one of the company's directors at the time Hancock resigned, "During Ellen's tenure, Exodus enjoyed phenomenal growth and was able to build a world-class data center infrastructure and managed services offerings, benefiting greatly from her technology expertise."[2] "Phenomenal" does not begin to describe the company's business expansion: Under her direction, Exodus enjoyed 400 percent annual growth each year from 1997 through 2000. She was entirely focused on growing the company.

Such narrowly focused determination had been the source of both Hancock's successes and her failures throughout her career. According to a profile published in *Business Week e.biz*, she had "a reputation as a fierce competitor and a straight shooter, ... running IBM's networking division and overseeing 15,000 employees" in the early 1990s.[3] However, according to the profile, "Hancock has never been considered a visionary. As IBM's networking chief, she saw Big Blue demol-

Men at once become fascinated by any extension of themselves in any material other than themselves. Understanding Media, 1964

ished in the emerging high-speed networking market by a then upstart called Cisco Systems Inc. She also was knocked at IBM for being slow to grasp the Internet."[4]

Managing a Hot business in a Hot industry easily EXTENDS success. However, in a super-heated industry, success REVERSES INTO failure with equal ease. A business that is narcissistically focused to the point of being numb to the warnings of the REVERSAL and RETRIEVAL quadrants can do no better than collapse with its industry.

> **A business narcissistically focused to the point of being numb to the warnings of REVERSAL and RETRIEVAL can do no better than collapse with its industry.**

Exodus Communications, led by Ellen Hancock, was consumed by its focus on growth. In fact, less than a year before its eventual demise, Exodus concluded a $6.5 billion acquisition of GlobalCentre, Inc., assimilating its forty-six worldwide data centres and 5,000 customers. From a talk she gave in Toronto shortly after that acquisition,[5] it seemed clear that Ellen Hancock saw the reflection of an ever-expanding Exodus in the McLuhanistic Hot-business fountain and was both enchanted and numbed by the vision. She sadly seemed unable to envision any other possibility for her business, including its eventual, and unfortunately inevitable, demise according to the Laws of Media and Media Temperature effects.

Generally speaking, a Hot business in a Hot industry will tend to over-heat and thus manifest the business's REVERSAL properties. Therefore, businesses in Hot industries should at least possess some Cool influences for management, if not become Cool businesses overall. The converse is often true as well: To capture customers' attention and spending in a Cool industry, the business must be Hot.

Fashion: Hot Cool-ture

Season after season, women's fashion is exceedingly Cool. Fashion is continually in flux, so that its aficionados and the "fashionistas" are constantly engaged by the latest showings of the major designers. Haute couture is about "the latest look" — visual — but it also extends the tactile through the variety of fabrics and textures and even the aromas of the latest *parfums*. Often, the female figure is partially, and hence seductively, revealed by the newest fashions, providing the relatively low definition that encourages engagement and higher mental participation. Haute couture is Cool.

The business of the fashion industry, however, is a study in Hot. Each business season is remarkably short and intense, with styles going out of fashion, usually before the current season's racks have been cleared. Depending on the particular clientele, the selling environment is designed to be completely immersing for the customer, whether it is the high definition of a designer's own shop, or the high volume, hip-hop audio overload that is characteristic of teen-oriented marketing. The market is also extremely fragmented and specialized, with corporations owning several retail chains, each catering to a very narrow, highly focused demographic.

To maintain the highly engaged customer, who may just as easily patronize a competitor as she would your business, the company must capture her attention. Indeed, the only commodity of true value in a Cool environment is attention — the result of a highly focused, short and intense experience. In other words, a Cool industry necessitates Hot experiences and Hot companies for an enterprise to succeed ahead of its rivals.

In a Hot industry, a Hot company risks burning out. In a Cool industry, the Cool company risks losing its customers' attention — and its customers.

Managers Hot and Cool

Individual managers can be Hot and Cool as well, with the temperature of the company often reflecting that of its senior management. Jack Welch, former CEO of General Electric Corporation, is a Cool manager. In an interview with Jeffrey E. Garten, the author of *The Mind of the CEO*, Welch said:

> The biggest change we made, without question, was the move to a boundaryless company. We got rid of the corner offices, the bureaucracy, the 'not-invented-here' syndrome. Instead, we got every mind

> When a thing is current, it creates currency; fashion creates wealth by moving textiles and making them ever more current. Understanding Media, 1964

in the game, got the best out of all our people. My main job was developing talent. I was a gardener providing water and other nourishment to our top 750 people.[6]

Welch naturally engaged his staff and tended to be inclusive, emphasizing active participation. Working to continually eliminate the fragmentation and procedural high definition that is characteristic of bureaucracy, Welch was able to achieve incredible efficiencies among his various businesses. His record of results over twenty years at the helm of a company as diversified as GE is unmatched by almost any other recent CEO. The culture he created at GE permeated his management team. Jeff Immelt, Welch's successor as Chairman and CEO reflects:

My style is that I look at every business from the outside in. My framework is very much the customer and outside market. ... I believe in people. I know the difference between a good one and a bad one. ... I love change. I love trying new things. I really bring to the job a complete growth headset.[7]

Immelt, like Welch before him, makes effective use of the multi-sensory organs of a corporation — the people. As we discovered earlier, a corporation is both literally and metaphorically an extension of man *in toto*. The executive who can use all his available senses and organs by delegating authority and effectively running an open, distributed organization is the Cool manager.

On the other hand, there is the senior manager who is authoritarian, single-mindedly focused only on that which interests him or her, and often overly "hands on." He or she is Hot. Such a manager is less likely to be flexible in his or her view of the business and open to new ideas. Hot managers require considerable convincing — high definition — before they will accept new concepts. New ideas and approaches represent new perceptions from the multiplicity of sensory organs throughout the corporation. They frequently require considerable "filling in" during their early stages of conception. These all represent characteristics that are foreign and possibly threatening to Hot managers as new views compromise their intense focus.

Cool management culture is typically more robust and resilient. Hot management culture is more singularly dependent on the leader.

Because of this, Cool management culture is typically more robust and resilient. Not only are Cool management teams better able to weather storms in the economy, they are likely better able to anticipate them as well. This is not to say that a Hot management culture cannot sustain sea changes in its business. However, Hot management culture is more singularly dependent on the leader, who invariably is strongly charismatic. Case in point: Bill Gates and Steve Ballmer of Microsoft — both Hot managers.

Microsoft

Gates is widely acknowledged as brilliant and possesses an inquiring mind. But, characteristic of a Hot personality, he has always focused single-mindedly on the scientific and technical subjects that interest him and on philanthropy, which is, more often than not, tied to his corporate endeavours. He rarely brooks interference or dissent from others in the pursuit of his objectives, all based on the certainty of his worldview and his unwavering conviction.

However, while Gates ran Microsoft, he did something uncharacteristic for a company with a Hot management culture: Microsoft employed a Cool manager as its Chief Technology Officer. Until his retirement, Nathan Myhrvold provided the forward sensing of impending changes that would affect the business. He was able to assimilate massive amounts of low-definition information and use it to heighten Microsoft's corporate awareness and perception. According to industry folklore and numerous anecdotes, Myhrvold exercised significant influence over Gates's views and decisions pertaining to critical, strategic issues.

There is little wonder, for example, that Microsoft's first Internet initiatives, strongly encouraged by Myhrvold, were exceedingly Cool. Despite the fact that their browser business strategy was highly aggressive and ultimately led to the antitrust suit brought by the U.S. Justice Department, Internet Explorer itself was compliant with open standards. It also incorporated support for competitor Sun's Java language and Microsoft Visual Basic's rival, JavaScript. Within Microsoft, resources and power shifted away from the operating-systems exec-

Leaders seek audiences. Emperors give audiences. Culture is Our Business, 1970

utives to favour those responsible for Internet-based initiatives. Compare this with Microsoft's .NET strategy, conceived after Myhrvold's retirement.

.NET enables fragmented use of software services by subscription and is characterized by a high degree of control by Microsoft over what companies are, and are not, included in the initiative. Various carrot-and-stick incentives were proposed to both potential partners and large, corporate customers in an attempt to promote the move to new operating software versions required by .NET. According to industry analysts and commentators, a clear pattern of fragmentation, isolation of those using prior versions and punitive exclusions is emerging. Quite literally, this architecture requires less "filling in" by the consumers, as name, passwords and even financial account information can be automatically maintained by a Microsoft .NET component, Passport. Within Microsoft, power has reverted to the traditionally strong operating-system factions. Without Myhrvold's Cool moderating influence, the Hot corporate culture returns to the fore.

Cultured Business

A business's culture is commonly considered as the subjective environment in which employees go about their daily corporate lives. It has been colloquially taken to refer to such traits as the manner of acceptable dress, whether there is a cappuccino maker in the company kitchen or how many levels of managerial signatures are required to purchase ink cartridges for printers. In the general case, however, corporate culture governs individual and collective behaviour and influences how business strategies are conceived and enacted.

The corporate culture is the Message of the corporation Medium.

It could be said that if a corporation is a Medium — and we know that it is an inclusive extension of many aspects of a person — then its culture is the collection of effects caused by, and through, the corporation. The corporate culture is the Message of the corporation Medium. A company's behaviour might therefore be better understood by applying the various principles of *figure* and *ground*, Hot and

Cool, and the Laws of Media. These will all assist managers in understanding a corporation's effects on all of its various participants through new awareness and insights. This is easier said than done… especially for a company insider.

McLuhan probed the effects of new Media, that is, all technologies and innovations that extend mankind, on culture and society. Probing and investigating allowed him to make his often astounding observations and predictions. He never claimed to have clairvoyant or precognitive powers. Rather, McLuhan maintained that the effects of a given Medium exist from its inception and their actions on society and culture had been well established by the time he made his observations. The effects went unnoticed by most people, McLuhan said, because they acted as a hidden *ground*. The general public was numbed by the effects of these new Media. Hence, people were unable to realize them until they were observable from the perspective gained by the passage of time — as McLuhan put it, through the rear-view mirror.

Although McLuhan was not immune to Media's effects himself, he was at least able to perceive them and, in most cases, able to distinguish a *ground* unnoticeable by others. By analogy, the same holds for corporations. Management and staff together experience the corporate culture, that is, the effects and changes caused by the corporation Medium, as a hidden *ground* and respond to it almost on an instinctual level. The first time many people are able to notice the effect the company has had on them is after they leave, even though it may have been plain to close friends and relatives. Sometimes, it is only when a particular aspect of the corporate culture is changed that staff notice that something is different, something is missing.

The people within a company evolve its corporate culture over time — they shape their tools. In turn, people are inexorably changed by the effects of the corporation and corporate life — thereafter their tools shape them.

In the McLuhanistic metaphor, corporate culture is the set of effects and changes in scale, pace and pattern caused by the corporation acting on its

Without an anti-environment, all environments are invisible. Culture is Our Business, 1970

people, customers and other companies. It can EXTEND, REVERSE INTO, RETRIEVE and OBSOLESCE constituents from a variety of categories:

- Ideas and ideals;
- Codes or modes of behaviour and mutual expectation;
- Ethics and sets of values;
- Language and conventions in speech, expression or conversation;
- History, mythology, legends, heroes and villains; and
- Traditions, commemoratives and celebrations.

Old Culture in New Bottles

A new company will install the framework and trappings associated with many of these items to establish a basic cultural *ground*. Often, new companies' leaders will attempt to emulate corporate cultures belonging to corporations that they admire, or to which they aspire. They hope that some of their role model's "secret stuff" will rub off on them. When IBM led the world of enterprise-wide computing, both its competitors and those who swam in IBM's wake adopted Big Blue's blue or grey suit, white shirt and red tie. More recently, foosball tables and cappuccino machines became Silicon Valley clichés throughout the high technology industry because early leaders among dot-com companies enjoyed such recreations and trifles. Styles of e-mail communication, the processes for accepting — or killing — new undertakings, management reporting cycles and requirements, the style and agenda for staff meetings are all arbitrarily conceived shortly after a company is founded.

New companies' cultural components are all *figures* cast against a multitude of *grounds* brought by the newly acquired staff. Everything is noticed so any attempt to change that freshly seeded culture is merely an exercise in changing overt procedures. Over a span of years, and certainly decades, individuals are changed by these collective actions and effects, inculcating respective responses and behaviours. The longer the culture has to steep, the more hidden the cultural *ground* becomes. Equally, the more difficult it becomes to change.

Because of this, outsiders coming into key positions in long-established companies can cause tremendous disruption in a very short time. For these relative newcomers, the corporation's hidden cultural *ground* is *figure* in high relief. It becomes an easy, obvious and inviting target on which to leave their marks, even if their common intention is simply to hang familiar and comfortable icons of their previous corporate cultures on the walls of their new corporate home.

The difference in perspective between a long-established corporate cultural *ground* and a new manager's cultural *figure* can sometimes work to the company's benefit if people recognize the need for radical, and noticeably disruptive, change. A sufficiently strong outsider, accompanied by a strong management team committed to the new leader's initiative, can use the culture Message to change the corporate Medium. For example, Lou Gerstner came to IBM when the computer industry superpower was rapidly in decline. He fundamentally changed major aspects of how the business was managed and how employees interacted. Gone were the blue suits and the revulsion for all things non-IBM. Gone, too, were the exclusive product-focused mentality, the self-perception of entitlement and even the country clubs. The cultural changes Gerstner instituted through the loyal and trusted management team that accompanied him allowed the company to regain much of its past success and glory.[8]

Carly Fiorina, CEO of Hewlett-Packard, has been less successful in attempting to change "the HP way" through moves to centralize internal management control and customer account coverage.[9] A procession of several Xerox senior executives have been profoundly unsuccessful in changing a decades-old culture whose defining nature seems to be resistance to change.[10] Clearly, changing a corporate culture is not as easy as merely handing down new marching orders.

The more deeply people participate in a culture, the less the motive for innovation.

From Cliché to Archetype, 1970

Changing the Corporate Culture

Understanding how to cause changes in the effects of a Medium are key to changing a corporate culture in a relatively short time. As we have seen, these techniques may include the following:

- Awareness-activating probes to assist in bringing aspects of a hidden *ground* into relief as *figure*. This approach is usually more effective in a relatively smaller and younger company with a willing complement of participants, or as a later phase of a larger initiative.

- Changing a Cool management style into a Hot one, but only for a short time. Such action conveys a sense of urgency to the initiative and causes intense focus with high definition. At the same time, it runs the risk of engendering resentment and revolt among those who previously played highly participative roles in a Cool culture. Reversing temperature may also permit the company to be blind-sided due to the reduction in its ability to sense diffuse, low-definition stimuli in its business milieu. The other danger is that it is difficult to go back. Cooling off a Hot Medium requires undoing its inherent numbing and fragmentary effects.

- Applying the Laws of Media tetrads to understand specific effects of the cultural components. Managers can then take active steps so that appropriate effects are reinforced and those less suitable for the desired result changed. By changing the Medium — the corporation — new effects will be initiated. It may be the case, for example, that some beneficial effects had once been OBSOLESCED. Management might decide to RETRIEVE them to cause the desired changes in corporate culture.

For each company's staff, the other's culture is a set of high definition effects that hits with the full force of a tidal wave.

When Cultures Collide

The problem of understanding and possibly changing corporate culture becomes even more urgent in the case of mergers and acquisitions. Imagine the turmoil that occurs when two large, well-established companies attempt to combine. For each company's staff, the other's culture is a set of high definition effects that hits with the full force of a tidal wave. What for one company is entirely *ground*, transforms to *figure*-without-*ground* for the other.

Conventionally, with respect to such cultural collisions, we can identify three possible outcomes. The first, and most common, consequence is the "victor/vanquished" model. One culture, usually that of the larger, acquiring company, dominates and the other culture is lost. Another possibility is that two strong cultures clash, sometimes for years, until a brand new composite culture emerges. A third eventuality is failure, as management's efforts are thwarted by the guerrilla actions of the old cultures' adherents.

However, our new awareness of a corporation's culture as the Medium's Message gives us a new tool. By applying the Laws of Media to the various cultural determinants of each company, we can begin to explicitly gain awareness of their effects. When considering two companies in the case of a merger or acquisition, comparing aspects of each respective quadrant for the companies' tetrads will allow management to perceive compatible and complimentary areas upon which they can build. It will also disclose potential inconsistencies or conflicts where attention must be paid to eliminate, or at least mitigate, the differences. One could say that management might be able to sense those circumstances which may be too Hot, those that might be too Cool and those that are just right.

Designing a Business from the *Ground* Up

Of course, every company works from its own *ground*, created by both the business conditions in which it exists, and the people who comprise the *corpus corporatus*. As the *grounds* for different companies are unique, so too are the hidden or unnoticed effects that influence them. Ideally, each company evolves uniquely. Its offerings will be developed in such a way that they will have unique twists or approaches to a market as management is able to perceive it. Effectively, every company will do something different.

However, in today's business reality, this is not the case. The influence of business schools' case-study approach, adopting so-called best practices discovered by others, and the ever-pressing need to "just get the job done," has a curious homogenizing effect that has become

> Man never intends the cultural consequences of any extension of himself.
>
> McLuhan Hot & Cool, 1967

the hidden *ground* for much of North American business. Companies will tend to move in parallel lines because of an artificial, often self-imposed, common ground. Old-line companies tend to play follow-the-leader, especially as senior executives who are successful in one context are recruited into another for a round of "lead the followers." New start-up companies experience a bandwagon effect that tends to be exacerbated in a Hot industry. For example, for a short time after Netscape issued its wildly successful IPO, browser companies were all the rage. Amazon.com's apparent success — at least for a relatively brief period in the stock market — begat online booksellers galore. Most of these boasted overall financial results akin to those of the only recently profitable Amazon, during the years before it finally realized what business it was really in.

> **Old-line companies tend to play follow-the-leader. Senior executives, successful in one context, are recruited into another for a round of "lead the followers."**

It is said that a person is truly insane if he or she repeats the same actions over and over, expecting a different result. If effective competition in business derives from differentiating oneself from others in the same market, what else can one call this attraction to 'follow the leader,' but a form of collective insanity? To be polite, one could call it being numbed by a Hot competitor.

Managers could alternatively take a Cool view of their respective, unique *grounds* and apply new tools to develop original thinking about a new business venture or opportunity. The movement and evolution of their companies should be more akin to Brownian motion, the independent movement of particles caused by collisions with molecules of the surrounding fluid medium. In business's case, the collisions with surrounding molecules are analogous to interactions with other companies, including competitors. There will be numerous unique approaches in the same market Medium, many of which could be complimentary to each other, rather than competitive.

And what does this change? When McLuhanesque thinking is applied in the context of developing businesses, the business's management team can discover new alternatives and approaches to existing markets. These could result in more choice to customers and consumers, and possibly the end of industrial age competition as we have known it, that is, as the hidden *ground* of the business paradigm.

Here are two companies that discovered unique, McLuhanesque approaches to their competitive business landscapes.

Shopping for a Story

Late in 2000, the market for online commerce infrastructure software technology was relatively crowded and dominated by major, well-funded young companies, primarily located in Silicon Valley. In addition, Microsoft, among other established companies, was developing similar software architecture components. Nonetheless, a small start-up company in Toronto, Canada developed its own electronic commerce infrastructure technology aimed squarely at this market.

Shopping ManuFactory

This company, which we will call "Shopping ManuFactory," created a structure that used Microsoft's standard Simple Object Access Protocol to transport software "objects" — packages of information — between centralized databases and the electronic commerce applications in which they were used. These objects contained such information as product specifications, pricing structure and associated business rules. Potentially, additional information and self-contained programming fragments could be added that would assist logistics and fulfillment applications, as well as provide product usage information, marketing collateral and promotions. Theoretically, there was no technological limit to the components of the information objects themselves.

In conjunction with the information object technology, the company also had developed a content management system by which the various objects were stored and maintained, and an order fulfillment application that allowed it to automatically source inventory and fill orders based on instructions received via the information objects.

Through various attempts to raise early stage funding, Shopping ManuFactory emphasized different aspects of its technology, all the while focusing on their uses and strengths. The trouble was that at each

In our electric age...we find ourselves at a loss to find the "rational"...because we never noticed whence it came in the first place. Understanding Media, 1964

meeting with a potential investor, the emphasis of the company's story "wasn't quite right," and so it was changed — repeatedly. The company became unable to articulate its true purpose and theme; like the mythical Narcissus, its management was seemingly numbed by the reflected perceptions of their technology's intrinsic capabilities and market potential.

It is clear that Shopping ManuFactory suffered from management's intensely Hot focus on the content of their Medium, as opposed to understanding its Cool Message. Here is an excerpt from the Laws of Media tetrad on the company's information object technology:

SHOPPING MANUFACTORY'S OBJECT TECHNOLOGY

EXTENDS

╌╌⫸ Ability to centrally manage and convey standardised product information, pricing, marketing collateral — central catalogue

REVERSES INTO

╌╌⫸ "Heavy" catalogues — inability to efficiently move any information across the network because of bloated objects

RETRIEVES

╌╌⫸ Brand management by manufacturers via active control and management of information, pricing, collateral, etc.

OBSOLESCES

╌╌⫸ Do-it-yourself online catalogues designed and developed by distributors/channels

Once again, the RETRIEVES quadrant provides the key to the tetrad. Prior to the 2001 crash of technology-based companies, electronic commerce — the facilitation of business transactions via the technologies and capabilities of the Internet — had been held out as the model for the future of modern business. "Eliminating the friction" in commercial transactions among corporate trading partners and the general public alike had been its promise. However, despite the promises and predictions, and with relatively few notable exceptions, e-commerce had evolved little beyond technology-enabled catalogue shopping and scaled-up versions of traditional commodity pricing skirmishes and market making.

Generally missed in the rush to implement clever electronic commerce technologies were many elements of sales and marketing — the cornerstones of commerce for centuries. The extreme emphases on advertising-fuelled branding, superficial database trickery or "Customer Relationship Management" systems are no substitute for highly prized vendor-customer relationships that ensure business loyalty and ongoing consistent revenue.

These relationships, at one time carefully nurtured and managed by the manufacturer or distributor, had been ceded to the retailer or market maker in an electronically-enabled marketplace. Unfortunately, these online retailers owe no fidelity to any particular brand, save their own. This loss of control by manufacturers was initially viewed by anarchically-oriented "Netizens" as a good thing: a transfer of power and control from the few to the many.

However, two inescapable truths were ignored in this process. First, any activity involving human beings — such as buying and selling — that does not consider human dynamics and the resultant effects may be efficient, but will not be entirely effective. Second, the previously mentioned transfer of market control meant that a large aspect of the manufacturers' ability to position and present their products was lost. Consequently, in the e-commerce model, the customer's buying experience is entirely owned and managed by a largely impersonal channel, aggregator or marketplace.

Any activity involving human beings that does not consider human dynamics may be efficient, but will not be entirely effective.

Shopping ManuFactory's e-commerce object technology returns control of product marketing — and hence, the customer relationship — to manufacturers, from a distributed and diverse channel. In other words, their technology provides those who have the responsibility to manage all of the information about a product or service the capability to do so. They would be able to maintain this ability regardless of where or how the products are represented, procured, sold or shipped. Further, the technology furnishes retailers an economical, consistent source of product sales and fulfillment information and capabilities. In a diverse, online shopping environment, the technology allows manufacturers to offer everything from audio and video commercials, through electronic discount coupons, to special quantity-discounted pricing, all encapsulated in the information object's "wrapper."

While it is non-trivial, Shopping ManuFactory's technology is not so unique that another company could not reproduce it. However, the company was able to differentiate itself in a crowded, competitive market through explaining the Message of its technology. Less than one year after being exposed to these new perceptions and insights of their business via our McLuhanesque thinking tools, management entered into a contract to sell the company, cashing out their financial and sweat equity investments.

Helping with Fifteen Minutes of Fame

As was the case with Shopping ManuFactory, many technology-based enterprises found their roots in a technological capability developed by programmers and engineers. Particularly where software or applications are involved, there is little in the technology that is truly unique, such that it cannot be replicated by another programming team. Indeed, during the expansion of what became known as the "Internet Bubble," a company with a relatively new software approach to a particular problem was quickly joined in the market by a host of potential competitors, all doing essentially the same things with their hot-off-the-workstation software.

PersonaMedia

A small, project-oriented software-development company wanted to commercialize an item from their technology portfolio, developed in the context of a larger project, but never actually used. To this end, they activated a previously incorporated entity called PersonaMedia with the primary purpose of commercializing what they called MySpeak™.

MySpeak provided the technical capability for a computer to answer an incoming phone call, capture a voice message, convert it to a streaming media object that was managed by a database and present it on a Web page — entirely without human intervention. What would typically take a person between one and two hours to accomplish manually could occur automatically in a minute or less, for thousands of calls per day. While the capability never failed to capture the attention of all who tried it, its technological underpinnings were not difficult algorithms, to say the least. One of the key issues the company had was positioning MySpeak, and creating a theme and objectives for PersonaMedia's business — what others might call its vision and mandate.

The founders decided to engage the authors' assistance to build PersonaMedia from the *ground* up, literally applying McLuhanesque thinking and approaches to the challenges of building a company. Over a period of weeks, during which time we also addressed conventional business planning activities like revenue and expense projections, development schedules, production considerations, equipment provisioning and so forth, we slowly built the Laws of Media tetrad for MySpeak, generically known as "Voice on the Web." (See page 168.)

When first introduced to MySpeak's capability, prospective customers are usually impressed by the "coolness" of the technology, as in "Wow! My voice is on a Web page. That's cool!" They, like PersonaMedia's competitors, focus primarily on the content of the Medium, in other words, its direct use. However, in designing and building the company, we were more concerned with the Message of the Medium: What changes in the customer's business could be effected by MySpeak? What changes will occur in our customers' relationships with their customers? What do these, in turn, change? For insights, we began our considerations in the key insight quadrant — RETRIEVES.

What changes in the customer's business could be effected by MySpeak? What changes will occur in our customers' relationships with their customers?

It soon became clear to us that the power of MySpeak lay in its ability to enable storytelling via the Internet: A person with some sort of tale or experience or information to share could do so via MySpeak, regardless of whether they were computer literate or had ready access to a networked workstation. Most technology-related companies focus on the relatively young, computer-savvy demographic. Our view was that MySpeak could enable at least inbound Internet access to anyone who could reach a telephone from somewhere in the world, at any time of the day or night.

VOICE ON THE WEB (MySpeak)

EXTENDS

- ...⟩ Diary / Immediate Journal[0]
- ...⟩ Presence[1]
- ...⟩ Community[2]
- ...⟩ Reach to non-computer savvy, offline or non-reading audience[3]
- ...⟩ Self-publishing or Vanity press[4]
- ...⟩ Immortality / Persistence[5]
- ...⟩ Broadcaster model (many to few to many)[6]
- ...⟩ Capture of oral / aural (business) information[7]
- ...⟩ Individual as "star"[8]
- ...⟩ "Knowledge Management" via ... [9]
- ...⟩ Understanding via conveying tone, emotion, mood, etc.[10]
- ...⟩ News reporting (instant, on-the-spot)[11]

REVERSES INTO

- ...⟩ Omnipresence / Big Brother[1]
- ...⟩ Free for all[2]
- ...⟩ Audience is the show[2]
- ...⟩ Narcissism[4]
- ...⟩ Clutter[5]
- ...⟩ Celebrity "becomes human"[0,8]
- ...⟩ Cacophony / noise[7]
- ...⟩ Icon / Idol or Cult of celebrity[0,8]
- ...⟩ Misunderstanding; hearing only the tone, not the words.[10]
- ...⟩ "Olds" (as opposed to "news") reporting; false news[11]
- ...⟩ News as a competitive / contact sport[11]

RETRIEVES

- ...⟩ Tribal Council[2]
- ...⟩ Town Crier[3,6,11]
- ...⟩ Oral tradition / Oral history[5,10]
- ...⟩ Storytelling (key to the appeal of the Internet)[3,6,7,10]
- ...⟩ ... Respect for history, past wisdom, insight[9]
- ...⟩ Role of the Archivist[5,9]
- ...⟩ Acoustic Space (omni-centred, no predetermined perspective, all points of view are valid)[7]
- ...⟩ Andy Warhol: "In the future, everyone will be famous for 15 minutes."[8]
- ...⟩ Literal manu-scripts / monographs / pamphleteers[6,11]
- ...⟩ "Roving Reporter"[8]

OBSOLESCES

- ...⟩ The fleeting, temporary, vanishing[5]
- ...⟩ Phone system broadcast voicemail[3]
- ...⟩ Written history[3,7]
- ...⟩ Transcription filtering / interpretation (by a possibly biased scribe)[3,4,7,10]
- ...⟩ Written literacy[3,7]
- ...⟩ Traditional broadcasters' model (few to many, and hence...)[6]
- ...⟩ Traditional producers[6]
- ...⟩ Cult of celebrity[8]

Armed with this insight, our business-development efforts expanded from companies that had an Internet focus to those that served people who typically did not have Internet access, but that desired their contributions, suggestions, comments and feedback. This allowed us to target companies for whom publishing travel or experience journals would be beneficial to business, for example. It also expanded our thinking to the realm of opinion surveys and screening interviews. We designed an offering that companies could use as a tightly focused management tool with which to gauge before and after effects of implemented business, facilities or process changes.

Over time, we considered what was the overall, long-term theme of PersonaMedia's business. We recognized from the EXTENDS quadrant and from the limitations of a phonetic alphabet noted by McLuhan, that orally-presented and aurally-received information is far richer than written information. We know, for example, that the contents of a sentence — the words —are limited in what they can communicate as compared to the richness of meaning that can be conveyed by tone of voice, inflection, nuance and mood. In a business context, when simple text is stashed away in a repository, it is only a partial message. The human context of the words, the author's mood and state of mind at the time, and any verbal clues as to intent, are forever lost.

We realized that regaining these rich aspects, and making them available in the context of business applications as useful information, would be potentially valuable for many companies. Thus, "Voice as a Rich Business Information Object" became the theme of PersonaMedia, and will govern long-term, strategic development initiatives.

From a tactical marketing perspective, the famous Andy Warhol quote, "In the future, everyone will be famous for 15 minutes," piques the interest of prospective customers. Its promise of fame, mentally connected with the prospect of having one's voice published on the World Wide Web, has been proven to be effective in attaining that most valuable of all commodities — attention. In addition, PersonaMedia's tag line slogan, "We'll be hearing from YOU!" used

It is in this way that audience participation is created. The spoken word involves all of the senses dramatically. Understanding Media, 1964

Cliché-to-Archetype probe sharpening to RETRIEVE and disarm the somewhat threatening cliché, "You'll be hearing from us."

Warning: Thinking Ahead

Once a company becomes established and moves into the sustainable growth phase of its existence, its managers tend to focus on growing the business through new or expanded product and service offerings, and on enlarging its market. Among larger companies, business strategists have the responsibility to consider forecasts of macro-economic and societal conditions and bring them to light. These forcasts are used to determine appropriate scenarios that could affect the company's growth and future viability. Typically, scenario planners project currently known correlative factors and apply the forecasted influences to the company's business plan. However, what is missed in this conventional approach are considerations of how our current tools and technologies change us in ways that are not predictable using normal forecasting methods. As McLuhan showed us, the ways in which our tools shape us have a far more profound effect on the future business climate than is generally acknowledged.

As an example, consider the message of the cell phone. Here is an excerpt from its tetrad that we discussed in Chapter 6.

CELL PHONE (Excerpt)

EXTENDS

···⋗ Independence, by not requiring "sitting by the phone, waiting for a call"[3]

···⋗ Accessibility, availability, and expectation thereof[4]

REVERSES INTO

···⋗ Being always "on call"[4]

···⋗ Expectation of immediate availability[3]

RETRIEVES

···⋗ Personal page or squire[4]

OBSOLESCES

···⋗ Solitude, isolation[2,3]

···⋗ "Down time"[4]

Many parents consider the cell phone to be a tremendous boon. No matter where they are, parents enjoy the confidence that their children can always reach them should an emergency or crisis arise. Children, equally confident in the fact that their parents are but a mere phone call away, feel secure: If a homework assignment is left at home, or they are caught without transportation or even locked out of the house, mom or dad are virtually close at hand. In fact, for many children, the knowledge that parents are almost always instantly available is a central part of their life conditioning — their *ground*.

Cell phone equals instant contact and availability. And what does this change? Children begin to rely on this knowledge and build expectations. Not only do they expect availability and an instant response — a worldview now reinforced by Internet email and Instant Messaging — they are also developing the expectation of assistance and rescue in times of trouble. In turn, becoming dependent on this mechanism reduces their perceived need to plan ahead or foresee potential predicaments. They become less reliant on planning, formality and structure as they become more conditioned to count on the easy bailout.

The first generation of children who grew up with near ubiquitous use of cell phones is now entering the work force. In the field of computer programming, we have observed a decrease in project management abilities and requirements specification. Concurrently, especially among the youngest programmers, there has been an increase in what is called, "extreme programming." Programmers, working with one or two partners, quickly code a needed programming segment and try it out. If it does not meet the user's requirements, the code is returned to the programmer, modified and sent back. After several quick iterations, the program may be deemed "close enough"

We shape our tools and thereafter our tools shape us. Understanding Media, MIT Press Edition, 1994

and the programmer moves on to the next segment. The programming partners check each other's work for obvious bugs, nominally hastening the debugging process, especially for persistent, thorny problems.

Instant programming. Instant access. Instant feedback. Instant bailout. We can readily observe the first effects of how the Messages of current tools — cell phones in this case — begin to affect and change the mentality and behaviour patterns of people and society. In computer programmers' prior years, there was an extreme emphasis on the disciplines of project management, requirements specification, building prototypes, extensive testing and integration. The Instant Generation tends to disregard many of these disciplines, considering them redundant compared to "just doing something."

> **Those industries that count on planning for their sustainability will undoubtedly be forced to change their business models.**

Consider the effects of lifetimes lived with minimal conditioning in favour of advance planning, as may be the case when this generation is middle aged. Those industries that count on planning for their sustainability will undoubtedly be forced to change their business models. The life insurance industry counts on years of collecting premiums to fund investments from which the inevitable payouts are made. Those whose life conditioning pays little heed to advanced planning in favour of instant response and availability of bailout do not neatly support the insurance industry's current business model. The retail financial planning industry, together with those companies that supply financial products, now counts on future-focused baby boomers to sustain its growth. That will all change within the next quarter-century as those who will then enter their peak planning years will have a conditioned aversion to planning. There will clearly be necessary changes to social security and social assistance within ten to fifteen years after that, depending on prevailing attitudes toward the social safety net. But, of course, consider who will comprise the majority of the electorate at that time.

Challenging Business Ethics

Looking ahead to the future begins with an acute awareness of the present. The tools that shape us, and our thinking, exist today. The forces that will create our future are the effects that these tools have on us, and our collective reactions to these effects. Of course, our reactions are unavoidably coloured by what is deemed to be acceptable to the society at large.

From time to time, both long-established businesses and new ventures will be dogged by these acceptability or ethical issues. In some cases, the issues will go to the very heart of the business's endeavours, threatening its viability by targeting products, services or its intrinsic business model. In other cases, a business may find itself in the line of fire, as it becomes associated with an event or Hot — intense, fragmenting and numbing — situation.

Business's responses to such predicaments have ranged from attempting to ignore the resultant protests, hoping they will pass, to actively mounting an offensive, believing that right — or at least the right of survival — is on its side. Neither position is entirely effective over the long term, nor productive in the short term.

Business's undertakings are rarely good or evil in the absolute. After all, a business has no soul or conscience: These quite intangible extensions of humankind manifest themselves in the business context only by virtue of individual employees' actions. When a company introduces a new product or pursues a line of research, it creates a Medium. We know that, rather than the content of the Medium or its use, the true power of the Medium is in its Message — the changes it can cause. In this respect, the Message of the Medium is truly objective with respect to its *ground*. It is neither good nor bad, proper nor improper, righteous nor malevolent. However, ethical considerations force a change to that *ground* when value judgements are applied to the Message.

........: People hope that if they scream loudly enough about "values" then others will mistake them for serious sensitive souls who have higher and nobler perceptions than ordinary people. McLuhan Hot & Cool, 1967

In business reality, ethical issues concerning a newly created Medium are Hot and can arise suddenly.

Ideas, too, are Media and as such, are subject to the Laws of Media. Concepts that we associate with values, as well as the defining frames that engender value judgements, could potentially be understood in this fashion. Religious beliefs, moralistic codes and various philosophies can be framed so that a dispassionate observer may discern the rationale of human reactions to a particular Medium when it is cast against one ethical *ground* or another.

Rarely, however, are ethical discussions dispassionate. In business reality, ethical issues concerning a newly created Medium are Hot and can arise suddenly. They are often the result of technological innovations, but also spring from the handling of unexpected events. In many ways, dealing with them resembles an old-fashioned Junior High School dance — those of one persuasion are lined up against one wall, those of the opposite persuasion are lined up against the other. Both sides glare uncomfortably at each other across a great divide, into which only the courageous venture to participate in an awkward frenzy.

Despite McLuhan's reminder that "value judgments create smog in our culture and distract attention from processes,"[11] managing ethical issues has become increasingly unavoidable. Especially with the rise in popularity of the anti-globalization and anti-capitalism movement, the affluent middle class among Western societies has exercised political clout that checks business's initiatives and ambitions. There are many who would exclaim, "And rightly so!" In some cases, justifications for the ethical conclusions to which societies jump are less clear.

Managers have an obligation to their businesses and to society at large to understand the complete effects — both positive and negative — of any new Medium that they may create — products, services, decisions and actions. In addition, their business responsibility extends to understanding the *ground* upon which value judgements imposed by opponents are based. Only then can managers begin to address the concerns in a way that encourages awareness among all parties as to what, in all likelihood, has become a controversy.

In addition, we have seen that a given Medium, no matter how apparently beneficent it may be, has characteristics that will REVERSE INTO an opposite effect under the right conditions. Certain current circumstances that are OBSOLESCED by the Medium may actually be desirable. Historical precedents could be cautionary counsel. Carefully and prudently navigating a potentially dangerous course is also an obligation of business managers.

Managers have an obligation to society at large to understand the complete effects of any new Medium that they may create.

Genetically Modified (Food) Organisms

Let us briefly consider some of the issues surrounding the practice of genetically modified food organisms. Agricultural science and business have learned to EXTEND in the laboratory what farmers have done for decades: Crossbreed different plants to produce a new species that has some of the beneficial characteristics of both. In the case of GM(F)Os, the new species are specifically engineered using technologies and cross-bred species that could not occur through natural and traditional breeding techniques. Fears range from the creation of uncontrollable "Franken-foods" with unknown health risks to business monopolies holding patents on the source of essential foodstuffs. Here is one version of a tetrad that examines the medium.

GENETICALLY MODIFIED (FOOD) ORGANISMS

EXTENDS

┄┈> Yield of crops via increased resistance to bad things (e.g., disease, insects)[1]

┄┈> Ability to enhance nutrient content of foods[2]
Both of these leading to improved nutrition in, e.g., underdeveloped nations (3rd world)

┄┈> Public fear via fear of unknown effects, past failings and unintended consequences of science[3]

┄┈> Rehabilitates certain crops by rendering them edible (via modification) or by using beneficial aspects as the modifying agent in another crop[4]

┄┈> Agribusiness's revenue and monopoly on nature through gene patents, control of seed crop, etc., thereby increasing public dependence on specific Agribusiness companies[5]

REVERSES INTO

┄┈> Decreased yield of crops as one "supercrop" dominates, or as decreased natural gene pool renders modified crop more vulnerable[1]

┄┈> Elimination of certain other nutrients or beneficial combinations[2]

┄┈> Hysteria and arbitrary imposition of restrictions due to popular misconceptions, leading to promotion of "junk science"

┄┈> Underground science, unchecked by ethics or public oversight/review; greater chance for unintended consequences[3]

┄┈> Creation of new organisms, not originally found in nature, with unknown properties (beneficial or detrimental)[1,2,4]

RETRIEVES

┄┈> Eugenics ("racial purity" and perfection) imposed on nature[1,2]

┄┈> Superstition, wrong conclusions, persecution of scientists (e.g., Galileo, Darwin)[3]

┄┈> Concept of reincarnation[4]

┄┈> Concept of vaccine, rendering a bad thing (virus) into a good thing[4]

┄┈> Big Tobacco, with ultimate government / public consequence[5]

OBSOLESCES

┄┈> Plant disease and pests[1]

┄┈> Human disease, potentially famine, malnutrition[2]

┄┈> Genetic diversity[1]

┄┈> Crops with no use (to humans) Q: are they useful in the ecology? If not, why/how did they survive/evolve?[4]

┄┈> Competition from non-patent-holding companies or from companies with "inferior" crops[5]

Throughout the tetrad, we can see numerous effects that can be judged as either beneficial or detrimental, depending on one's point of view and individual politics. As is the case with other Media, GM(F)O's effects suggest issues that are reflected by multiple opinions from both sides of the "dance." The problem is that all of the effects are present simultaneously. All sides can offer persuasive and valid arguments, simply because all aspects co-exist in the Medium as complementary components.

Neither side can argue the inevitability of any particular effect to justify its position: Because of a Medium's multi-faceted effects, no specific doomsday or utopian scenario is more or less likely than another. However, careful consideration and our new McLuhanistic insight provides us with an "early warning" system that is strongly indicative in nature. The four Laws of Media can warn of consequences, which may, in the collective wisdom of society, be considered undesirable. However, compound consequences in life are rarely that clear. Let's consider one possible scenario.

Suppose GM(F)Os are used to increase the yield of food production under marginal agricultural conditions, and thereby increase the effective arability of land. Assuming potable water is also available, this changes the availability of the most basic of needs — food for what now are starving masses living in abject poverty throughout the Third World. These people can slowly increase their standard of living. Mere survival no longer commands total attention.

As has occurred in many other developing countries, the people, once emancipated from hunger, become a source of relatively inexpensive labour. However, their labour may not necessarily be directly exploited by the West. Rather, they may be employed by those countries that supply such labour forces today, their domestic workforces having become, in relative terms, expensive. Industrialization of the Third World ensues. And what does that change?

On the one hand, the beneficial consequences may include: increased education and literacy throughout the Third World to support new industrialization; increased economy and trade with the subsequent creation of a middle class; decreased willingness to

Moralistic expression of approval or disapproval is currently being used in our world as a substitute for observation and study. McLuhan Hot & Cool, 1967

compromise a new, relatively affluent lifestyle for ideology and hence a reduction in global violence, terrorism, revolution and strife.

On the other hand, among those items that may be seen as deleterious are: loss of habitat and further depletion of oxygen-producing rain forest through industrial development; continued extinction of species because of loss of habitat; pollution and the subsequent depletion of natural resources; and job loss in the populous, newly industrialized nations of South Asia and the Far East.

Being aware of these effects gives us the opportunity — and the responsibility — to manage ourselves, our technology and our world.

We are not predicting either of these sets of scenarios. They are all potential consequential effects of one aspect of allowing the proliferation of certain GM(F)Os. Nonetheless, being aware of these effects gives us the opportunity — and the responsibility — to manage ourselves, our technology and, to the extent that we can, our world.

Let's consider a different scenario. Suppose public fear, outrage and worldwide boycotts at the supermarket effectively shut down legal or sanctioned GM(F)O research and production. Carried to the extreme, the advancement of science that GM(F)O technology represents REVERSES INTO a scientific "chill." This could be implemented by withholding research funding, government grants and potential venture investments due to legislative lobbying by influential non-government organizations, environmentalists and certain religious interests. Conceivably, successes by these groups on the GM(F)O front will embolden them to expand an anti-science agenda that could lead to persecution of scientists. Advanced scientific research that may be controversial could subsequently be forced underground.

This scenario is actually quite plausible. Recent government policies in the United States with regard to stem cell and other genetic-based research indeed suggest such a direction may be the actual intention of the George W. Bush administration.[12] And what does this change? We have already seen a rise in anti-science legislation pertaining to education in many locales throughout the U.S. This, in turn, leads to a decrease in the development of critical thinking skills among students and the inability to form objective hypotheses. There is a definite increase in superstition among Western, industrialized populations and an increasing tendency toward religion as public policy in many developed countries. By choice, this scenario has our civilization RETRIEVING the Dark Ages and the pre-Enlightenment period in Europe, moving backwards into the future.

Until now, most of the debate surrounding GM(F)Os has centred on relatively near-term effects. However, looking beyond the immediately recognizable effects on the next few harvests, as we have just done, seems to cast the ethical issues related to Genetically Modified (Food) Organisms in a somewhat different light.

8.
"Humpty Dumpty Together Again"

Connected Intelligence in the Organization

"Unlike the old specialism,
contemporary forms of human employment
demand the creative
powers of design
through
pattern recognition
and inclusive social
awareness."

—Take Today: The Executive as Dropout, 1972

This inclusive social awareness is part of what McLuhan called "Humpty Dumpty put together again,"[1] that is, the tendency of electricity to reverse all the fragmenting effects of the Mechanical Age and the Industrial Era into integration and inclusion. He thought that "all the king's horses and all the king's men" that "couldn't put Humpty Dumpty together again" were just a bunch of specialists. "This is the point about the King's horses and men," McLuhan writes in *Understanding Media*, "They, too, are fragmented and specialized. Having no unified vision of the whole, they are helpless."[2] He compared the effects of electricity to the replaying of a film reel backwards. As he observed, "electricity compels us to play our mechanical development backward, for it reverses much of that development."[3]

> Energy and production now tend to fuse with information and learning. Marketing and consumption tend to become one with learning, enlightenment, and the intake of information. This is all part of the implosion that now follows or succeeds the centuries of explosion and increasing specialism.[4]

The broken egg is made whole again by reversing this process of history. Throughout this book, we have addressed the question of improving the manager's thinking with the help of some of McLuhan's best tools. In this concluding chapter, we want to propose ideas and tools to improve the whole company's thinking. While it is not possible to really control knowledge, creativity and innovation in one's company, it is certainly within reach to facilitate and improve them. McLuhan is helpful here too in that he recommends that we try to see the organization as an organic unity, much in the way our central nervous system unifies our whole body as a single operating environment.

> Our central nervous system is not merely an electric network, but it constitutes a single unified field of experience. ... The brain is the interacting place where all kinds of impressions and experiences can be exchanged and translated, enabling us to react to the world as a whole. Naturally, when electric technology comes into play, the utmost variety and extent of operations in industry and society quickly assume a unified posture.[5]

Company as Information System

In this way McLuhan invites us to rethink the nature of the company. In *Take Today: The Executive as Dropout*, he suggests that under the influence of computerization, an organization can be reintegrated and reharmonized, as if it were a musical instrument, so to speak.

> Under the influence of computerization, an organization can be reintegrated and re-harmonized, as if it was a musical instrument.

> ...a business operation at whatever level, whether in design, production, sales, distribution, promotion, or general management, can be conducted from a computer console. As with the old electric keyboard organ, from which the metaphor 'console' is borrowed, the computer console can extend simultaneously its chords, harmonies, and controls to a diverse number of areas of operation.[6]

And he adds this stunning conclusion: "More and more, the mind and the heart go into the musical score that determines the quality of business service or activity."[7]

In "Images of Organization," a remarkable analysis of how much the success or failure of companies can depend on the image they have of themselves, business consultant and professor, Gareth Morgan, proposes a less daring, and also more conventional metaphor for business operations.

> Organizations are information-systems. They are communication systems. And they are decision-making systems. We can thus go a long way toward understanding them as information-processing brains.[8]

After almost three decades of brain clichés, the comparison would be banal, but for the brilliant extension Morgan gives to this metaphor.

> The various job, departmental, and other divisions within an organization do not just define a structure of work activity. They also create a structure of attention, information, interpretation, and decision-making that exerts a crucial influence on an organization's daily operation.[9]

One wonders whether this structure of attention, information and so on — in other words, the intelligence of an organization — can be trained. Gareth Morgan asks: "Is it possible to design 'learning organizations' that have the capacity to be as flexible, resilient and inventive as the functioning of the brain? Is it possible to distribute capacities for intelligence and control throughout an enterprise so that the system as a whole can self-organize and evolve along with emerging challenges?"[10] His answer is yes. His vision of the organization is analogous to that of a hologram, in which all the information is contained in some measure in all the parts of the company. He proposes five principles:[11]

1. The "Whole" into the "Parts" principle, where the vision, the values and the culture established by the organization operate like a kind of "corporate DNA." This is partly achieved by providing a unified corporate style to all the employees.

2. The "redundancy" principle. This is not the same thing as the dreaded duplication of services and functions, but a strategy whereby several different people can be called upon equally to do the same thing at the time of need.

3. The "requisite variety" principle. This is the complementary opposite of redundancy whereby the organization needs to ensure as much diversity within its ranks as it is likely to confront in the environment or market in which it operates.

4. The "information underload" principle. Management should provide the minimum amount of specifications and target definitions, but no more, so as to interfere minimally with the innovative spirit in the company.

5. The "learning to learn" principle, that is, the capacity for the organization not only to practice and replay or "remember" what it has learned, but also to stay alert to the ever-changing conditions of its own operation. This may be the harder task; it would almost require a "scouting" position in the company.

These principles would serve to help Cool down a Hot company. As we noted in Chapter 6, some of the attributes of a Cool Medium include a tendency to include (principle 1), favouring generalization (principles 2 and 3), providing less information to encourage engagement and active participation (principle 4) and heightened awareness and perception (principle 5).

Unfortunately, many companies tend not to follow these guidelines. Individual departments or divisions often develop as autonomous entities unto themselves. They frequently seek to zealously guard their turf while they fragment the company and grapple with one another for influence, power and budget. As a result, when it comes time for the company to consider a major innovation or initiative, each department brings its own *ground* or context to the exercise. Rather than viewing the new Medium as a single *figure* against a common *ground*, the company ends up with a Medium cast against many distinct, fragmented grounds. Under such circumstances, it is almost impossible even to begin to understand or anticipate the effects, let alone manage so that desirable effects can be achieved. Clearly, some new form of constructive collaboration among the various departments and their staff is required.

> **Under such circumstances, it is almost impossible to begin to understand the effects, let alone manage so that desirable effects can be achieved.**

Shared Cognition: It's for the Birds!

Shared Cognition is the total field of understanding and planning that occurs in social groups. While we readily agree that humans routinely practice collaborative activities to obtain what they want, we also note that such activities might actually — and literally — be a more natural approach than individual actions. In fact, they may extend beyond socialized humanity. Consider this anecdote that was witnessed by one of the authors, de Kerckhove, while still a child, living with his parents at a United Nations residence in Peshawar, Pakistan:

> We had a friendly German shepherd that was fed outdoors. The meal consisted usually of large chunks of red meat in an earthen dish placed by the house bearer on the patio. One day, because the patio was filled with furniture while the house was being cleaned, the bearer put the dog's food in the garden a few metres away from the house. As usual, there were a group of three to four big black crows on the roof of the house. They were clearly interested in the dog's food. One of the crows flew to the ground in the garden to taunt the dog at a safe distance. As the dog abandoned his dish to make for the bird, another crow flew right over the dish and snatched a tasty morsel, thereby throwing the dog into a fit. In spite of the dog's rage or perhaps because of it, the crows managed to repeat the operation one more time. The whole thing came together for me when I noticed that all four birds were actually sharing the meat on top of the roof.

Where in a birdbrain did the crows plan this brilliant strategy? How did they plan it? Did they talk about it? Shared cognition — thinking and acting together, as it were — may not be limited to humans. It appears that the crows' behaviour was not part of a regular routine, or merely the result of some kind of self-organized happenstance, but the application of a real plan, entailing logical deductions and different stages of implementation. That stream of intentional intelligence involving communication and feedback between several members of a community, human or animal, is what we call Connected Intelligence (CI).

Connected Intelligence

Connected Intelligence is what we know as intelligence, but shared between people. Its principal Medium is speech. Talking is the standard way people "think together." People in groups share intelligence naturally without being aware that they are doing it. We call it conversation or discussion or brain-storming. CI expresses itself as the flow of thought and talk. There are as many forms of CI as there are purposeful human associations to work things out together. A classroom lecture or a boardroom meeting bring out different patterns of CI. A stage presentation or a movie organize people's emotions and thoughts in different conditions.

CI adds a new level of awareness about the process. This awareness helps to focus, organize and accelerate the process.

CI is intentional and focused. When people get together to solve a problem, make a decision or design a plan, they connect their intelligences. In any situation involving people working together, it is useful to discern the patterns arising from their collaboration: CI is an emergent property of the process. Even if they do not talk, people share the understanding of situations and contexts in intelligent ways. The difference is that CI adds a new level of awareness about the process. This awareness helps to focus, organize and accelerate the process. CI is both theory and practice. It aims at discovering and implementing disciplined ways of thinking together. The discipline consists in positioning people in relationship to each other so that each person's unique skill is given maximum play in a collaborative task.

CI is not subjective, but inter-subjective. It is based on the interplay of the participants' agendas and purposes, on the proper balance between connectivity and identity, individual knowledge and skills. Conventionally, internal tensions and unclear agendas block the flow of the process and reduce its effectiveness. Understanding CI helps to remove the blockage and refine the process. In the best of cases, appropriate connectivity comes naturally and leads quickly to exciting solutions shared by all participants.

Earlier in the book we wrote of how different groups within a company will bring their own *ground* to the understanding of any new Medium. While this is, of course, natural — each functional area of a typical corporation brings with it its own context — it is also terribly fragmenting. A Medium will certainly have numerous effects, and we have seen that it is entirely beneficial to understand them through the Laws of Media and Media Temperature. However, our understanding relies completely on our abilitiy to become aware of the possible effects with respect to the numerous *grounds* against which the Medium will eventually be cast. By probing the Medium from the respective *grounds* of individual departments, we impose the very corporate functional fragmentation whose influence we seek to overcome.

On the other hand, it becomes terribly impractical and unwieldy to attempt to understand the nature and effects of a new Medium from every possible *ground* at the same time. Within a company, this becomes a problem of having individual pockets of awareness, with the *corpus* of the corporation remaining asleep. Our true objective is to find a mechanism whereby the increased awareness, perception and insight can first be effectively shared, and then magnified, by the synergistic effects of combining multiple intelligences.

Connected Intelligence Playshop

McLuhan gives us a clue of how to accomplish this. He writes, "Any process that approaches instant interrelation of a total field tends to raise itself to the level of conscious awareness."[12] In the game of Connected Intelligence that we propose, we have created a framework

No medium has its meaning or existence alone, but only in constant interplay with other media. Understanding Media, 1964

in which "interrelation of a total field" — the Medium cast against multiple *grounds* — can be accomplished. Admittedly, it is not as instant as thoughts travelling at the speed of light. But certainly it is sufficient for the company to act as if it were approaching "conscious awareness."

Among several experiments to refine connectivity, we have developed the method of "Connected Intelligence Playshops" (CIP) to address issues, problems, strategies, crises and other challenges affecting different organizations ranging from an Ontario Elementary School association to business strategy development and national concerns in Canada, Italy, France, Portugal and the Netherlands, as well as business and government organizations in Australia, Argentina and Japan.

How CIP Works

The CIP is based on a simple formula — bringing together a mix of experts and non-experts, along with clients and business contacts, for a collaborative session in which each member has a specific role to choose and to play. The ideal number of participants is between fifteen and fifty. We have observed over the years that to tackle an issue and bring out the maximum of pertinent inputs from the participants, it is futile to mass them all together around a board table and simply take notes of what they say. The best method is to divide them into smaller groups, each exploring a different, but complementary, part of the problem at hand.

For instance, to give direction to the group, we can offer some of these basic questions:

- What business are we actually in, and is it the right business?

- Can we create fundamentally new products and services and what would be their effects?

- Can we redefine the boundaries between different industries and services so that new niches emerge? If so, what would that change?

- Can we structure our organization around business processes that are better aligned with the effects we want to have on our customers

Any process that approaches instant interrelation of a total field tends to raise itself to the level of conscious awareness. Understanding Media, 1964

rather than the influence of traditional departmental structures? How would that affect our corporate culture?

- Can we redesign business processes in a way that will better serve the business we are actually in? And what does that change?

The challenge is to first allow ideas to develop in each group. Then allow both the ideas *and the contexts from which they emerged* to circulate from group to group.

The prelude to the Connected Intelligence Playshop involves exposing all participants to McLuhan's thinking tools. Typically, this can be accomplished within an hour-and-a-half under the tutelage of a senior facilitator, using various short playshop examples, with table-groups in a large room. The large group is then divided into smaller groups of no fewer than five and no more than ten people, each being sent into separate rooms. To ensure the quality of discussion and adequate circulation of ideas, there should be a minimum of three groups, hence the lower limit of fifteen participants for an effective CIP. The ideal combination is to distribute fifty people in five groups of ten.

For the next hour, each group applies probes, the Laws of Media, Media Temperature and their understanding of *figure* and *ground* to the Medium under consideration. They are assisted and guided by a trained, "gentle" facilitator who encourages the discussion, and provides help with the McLuhanistic tools.

Individual roles in the groups may depend on the specific objectives of the exercise. If there is to be a formal report or presentation, there may be individuals who have specific responsibilities for various aspects of production. There may simply be one or two notetakers. However, in addition to the facilitator (who should not be one of the participants), each group must have two people playing the key role of "connectors." It is through the connectors that the power of Connected Intelligence is effected.

At the end of the hour, the two connectors depart for another group, carrying with them the collective wisdom of the first hour. A pair of connectors coming from a different *ground* joins each group and begins the next round by sharing tetrads, views on Media Temperature and the like with their new group.

Including a brief break between sessions, this intermezzo period should last no longer than about twenty minutes. After that, the newly formed group goes at it again, this time influenced by the introduction of a different *ground* and different tetradic sets of effects. The second round lasts another hour, at the end of which two new connectors depart for another group. The sharing process is repeated and one more hour-long session is held.

At the end of the session, all the groups meet once again in the large room to share their insights and discoveries. While the day is intensive, the entire process, from initial training to final sharing, can be accomplished in about six-and-a-half to seven hours, well within the time parameters of a business day.

To facilitate the flow of intelligence it is important that there are two connectors carrying the Messages from one group to another, so that we can be sure that few, if any, important ideas or insights are missed. Placing no fewer than five people in each group — although six is a better minimum — ensures that there is at least one person in each group who was there from the beginning. Further, employing new connectors for each round encourages participants to carry the newly synthesized *ground* and effects, as opposed to the *ground* of a prior round.

For more targeted objectives requiring a finished product at the end, there are additional roles in the CIP. In each group, participants can select from among roles that may include animator, producer, implementer or presenter. In larger groups, some roles can be doubled, for example, those of the connectors and presenters. All the roles are purposely simple so that anybody can adopt any one without training. While simple, the roles are important for several reasons: they give each participant a position, a function and a responsibility within the group; they also allow for the management of specific configurations and patterns of association between the groups. The producer, for example, is in charge of selecting and building the format in which the final product of the group's work will be presented. The role of the implementer is to verify the feasibility of the strategy and identify and list potential support for the projects in the real context of the strategy's implementation.

Tips for Playing Well

We offer some suggestions to achieve the best collaborative approach in a CIP.

1. Prior to the playshop, the stakes and the issues of the problem at hand must be teased out, parsed into distinct themes for each group and properly exposed and documented.

2. It is critical in a CIP to have a mix of experts and non-experts in any given field.

3. Of primary importance is to make each participant aware of CI as an added value. People will contribute more effectively to the common thinking activity if they recognize the nature of the process.

4. Participants need to choose and know their role, their task and their position in the process.

5. Depending on the circumstances, it is often necessary to work with a deadline. This may be useful as, in any cognitive process, there is a need for "closure," failing which the process may never reach a conclusion.

6. It is valuable, although not always indispensable, to have instant access to online resources both for research and collaboration.

7. The outcomes must be thought of as tangible, concrete results. In other words the solution proposed must be applicable as well as pertinent and valuable.

8. The results need to be expressed in a recognizable format so that they are accessible to those who did not participate in the CIP.

9. The results need to become independent from the process and thus exportable. This is a challenge to introduce clarity and comprehensiveness, as well as to remove the process jargon from the results.

The first step is to identify the problem or the task at hand. In the island of Madeira, where we conducted over a dozen such playshops, our job was to help the Ministry of Education of the Autonomous Region of Madeira to upgrade the local school system, technically and pedagogically, so that the students would include new media and online skills in their curriculum. The intention was to provide the next generation of Madeirans with new employment opportunities and include Madeira (population 250,000) in the global networked economy. Several CI playshops were thus conducted in Funchal, the capital of the island, and also in Toronto. Their purpose was to develop an overall strategy for the installation of the proper technical infrastructure and to obtain the Educational Ministry's buy-in for the administration and the training of educational personnel. Overall, the playshops were highly successful in bringing a rapid change of strategy in forty-five schools on the island.

The playshops were highly successful in bringing a rapid change of strategy in forty-five schools.

The idea of CI comes from the increased connectivity that networked media bring to people. That is why CI can work online as well as face-to-face. There is thus a CI technology implicit in all groupware and networking systems. Communities of practice develop from a common purpose, guided by the biases of a mental rather than physical proximity. To promote CI, software may not be always required, but it often helps the process, particularly for geographically dispersed organizations. In that respect, there is a significant difference between collaborative software that merely allows people to share in the management of documents, and software that allows them to share and exploit each other's ideas and inputs.

To facilitate the continuation and the refinement of collaboration online, we have developed software that enables the input of comments, suggestions and even audio-visual documents in named forums directly from chat modes. But even with the most basic of "instant messaging" systems available on the Internet, the concepts of Connected Intelligence can be effected in virtual presence.

The merit of this architecture of intelligence is that the connected thinking process occurs in stages, alternating between analysis and synthesis from the various interactions in the online forum. The key element to remember is that the process allows the unfettered appropriation of everybody's inputs to combine into a single production reflecting the original approach of each individual user. All this makes for an interesting new configuration of human memory in action, with different parameters, that now also includes intelligent processing and connecting.

We have tested the software very successfully with several hundred students to develop and articulate class projects. There is a potential to implement it for a major nation-wide initiative to bring students' resources, ideas and expertise together in small groups to identify and work on local, regional or national problems and issues. While still in the early developmental stages, there are already half a dozen projects under way, including a nation-wide initiative to create an online journal for students' projects.

The Effects of Connected Intelligence

What are some of the effects of Connected Intelligence? The following tetrad may help spur some of your own thoughts about what effects you may be able to cause in your organization.

CONNECTED INTELLIGENCE

EXTENDS / AUGMENTS / ACCELERATES

- Private and internalized cognition (private rumination)
- Connectivity
- Collaborative practices
- Networks (we make those tools and those tools shape us)
- Average I.Q.

REVERSES INTO

- Externalized cognition (dumping our minds as software on the Web, via Internet, cell phones and on all manners of screens)
- Discontinuity
- "Just-in-time" communities
- Co-opetition
- Lower than average I.Q.

RETRIEVES

- Context (what business are we in?)
- Pow Wow (collective ruminations)
- Swarming strategies
- Shared Cognition (roles)
- Group awareness

OBSOLESCES

- Text
- Hierarchy, Command and Control
- Broadcast modes
- Some level of privacy
- Some boundaries

Connectivity brings the collaborative, along with the competitive, edge. CI respects both. The identity of each participant is not ignored by the process but supported and given attention. Using CI in a classroom, for example, identifies and brings out the skills of each individual student, but for a common purpose, not just a private goal. Using CI in a boardroom helps to promote the feeling of a common purpose over and above the private goals of each member. It is also an ideal way to introduce new members, or new teams or new themes to an established, but not entrenched, group or company.

> **Using CI in a boardroom helps to promote the feeling of a common purpose over and above the private goals of each member.**

Hence, entering a company is akin to entering a large pool of cognitive resources, and quite literally being immersed in a community of practice. The field is very large, as it encompasses not only the individuals participating in a process, but also the Media and the total environment in which, and with which, the process occurs. For example, a football is a cognitive tool even as it focuses the attention of competing teams, and the intensely participating public on the shared cognitive environment that is the football field. In fact, team sport situations lend themselves well to comparisons with group cognition and, for that reason perhaps, they also provide many clichés and metaphors to CEOs when they want to instill unity in their enterprise.

Connected Intelligence is a huge but untapped resource within a company. The benefits of the Connected Intelligence Playshop are precisely that it can be structured to achieve faster and better results than conventional brainstorming sessions or simple lateral thinking exercises. In addition, it is one of the few, if not the only, techniques that ensure a common frame of reference — a common *ground* — at its conclusion among many diverse functional areas within a company or large organization. The CIP provides an effective approach that makes it possible to multiply mind by mind instead of merely adding mind to mind. By unleashing this newfound force within a company, the organization loses its fragmented linear, hierarchical, *visual* orientation. In its place, the McLuhanesque company assumes the characteristics of McLuhan's "acoustic space ... a resonant sphere whose center is everywhere and whose boundaries..." — and we would add, limitations, — "...are nowhere."[13]

⋯⋋ The matter is a perfectly trivial one... but there are points in connection with it which are not entirely devoid of interest and even of instruction. Sir Arthur Conan Doyle, *The Adventure of the Blue Carbuncle*

The End of the Beginning

The German philosopher Arthur Schopenhauer wrote, "An independent mind will think things that no one else can think about those things which everyone else already sees."[1] We advocate the creation of millions of independent business minds, all applying themselves to the challenging problems of business, culture, ethics and society. The obvious approaches and answers — "those things which everyone else already sees" — have been discovered and repeatedly applied. In many instances, these approaches are effective and are completely appropriate. We do not necessarily encourage reinventing wheels that will simply transport us along well-paved roads.

McLuhan would have us probe: What about square wheels? Triangular wheels? Octagonal wheels? He would have us consider these *figures* relative to the *ground* of perhaps not-so-well-paved roads, and how their use may effect change in our world. He would have us contemplate their tetradic nature, and from there, encourage our minds and imaginations to take flight, noticing something new about our world and our role within it. He reminds us that, "Embryonically, all problems contained all answers when one could discover a means of rendering them explicit."[2]

We cannot predict the future; we can only observe the present. We cannot know with complete certainty which Message of a given Medium will dominate, and which will have less importance at a given time in an arbitrary circumstance. In fact, except perhaps in matters of religious faith, we do not want to have complete certainty, for with certainty comes the permission to deny awareness and eliminate perception. With certainty, the future has already occurred, and we are merely riding backwards into it.

Business must embrace uncertainty and stare hard at the present. What haven't you noticed lately? What effects are happening right now, at this very instant? How are we being shaped and changed by the things and ideas which are all of our own making — all extensions of our abilities and consciousness beyond the physical confines of our bodies and minds? We urge business leaders to heed our final Message: "There is absolutely no inevitability as long as there is a willingness to contemplate what is happening."[3]

Notes

Introduction

1. Personal communication with D. de Kerckhove.
2. Marshall McLuhan and Barrington Nevitt, *Take Today: The Executive as Dropout* (New York: Harcourt Brace and Janovich, Inc., 1972), p. 16.
3. Marshall McLuhan, *Understanding Media: The Extensions of Man* (New York: McGraw Hill, 1964), p. 7.
4. Eric Norden, "A Candid Conversation with the High Priest of Popcult and Metaphysician of Media," *Playboy* (March 1969).

Chapter 1: Culture Is Our Business

1. Richard Pollack, "Understanding McLuhan," *Newsweek*, February 28, 1966, pp. 56–57.
2. Marshall McLuhan "A McLuhan Symposium," *The Antigonish Review*, 1988, p. 119.
3. See, for example, Philip Marchand, *Marshall McLuhan, The Medium and the Messenger* (Cambridge: The MIT Press, 1998), or Barrington Nevitt and Maurice McLuhan, eds., *Who Was Marshall McLuhan?* (Toronto: Stoddart, 1995), or W. Terrence Gordon, *Marshall McLuhan: Escape into Understanding, A Biography* (New York: BasicBooks, A Division of Harper Collins Publishers, 1997).
4. Glenn Willmott, *McLuhan or Modernism in Reverse* (Toronto: University of Toronto Press, 1996), p. 142.
5. Philip Marchand, (1998), op. cit., p. 109.
6. Ibid., p. 109.
7. W. Terrence Gordon, *Marshall McLuhan: Escape into Understanding, A Biography* (New York: BasicBooks, A Division of Harper Collins Publishers, 1997), p. 169.
8. Tom Wolfe, *The Pump House Gang* (New York: Farrar, Straus & Giroux, 1968), pp. 133-170.
9. Donald Theall, *The Virtual McLuhan* (Montréal & Kingston: McGill-Queen's University Press, 2001), p. 87.
10. Ibid. p. 87.
11. De Kerckhove's personal communication with McLuhan. McLuhan probably adapted this response from movie producer Sam Goldwyn, whom he quotes as saying, "As for movie critics, don't even ignore them." See Marshall McLuhan and Barrington Nevitt, *Take Today: The Executive as Dropout* (New York: Harcourt Brace and Jovanovich, Inc., 1972), p. 143.
12. Tom Wolfe, "What If He Is Right?" *The Pump House Gang* (New York: Farrar, Straus & Groux, 1968), p. 143.
13. Tom Wolfe, "A McLuhan Symposium," *The Antigonish Review*, 1988, p. 121.
14. Molinaro, McLuhan and Toye, *Letters of Marshall McLuhan*, (Toronto: Oxford University Press, 1987), p. 506.
15. John Cage, "A McLuhan Symposium," *The Antigonish Review*, 1988, p. 125.
16. Gordon (1997), op. cit., p. 97.
17. Marshall McLuhan in Gerald Emanuel Stearn, *McLuhan Hot & Cool* (New York: The Dial Press, Inc., 1967), p. 268.
18. Ibid.
19. Marshall McLuhan, *The Mechanical Bride: Folklore of Industrial Man* (Boston: Beacon Press, 1967).
20. Ibid., p. v.
21. Ibid.
22. George Sanderson and Frank MacDonald, eds., "Media and the Inflation Crowd," *Marshall McLuhan: The Man and His Message* (Golden, CO: Fulcrum, 1989), p. 61.
23. Interview with Marshall McLuhan, *The Antigonish Review*, 1988, p. 32
24. McLuhan and Nevitt (1972), op. cit., pp. 27-85.
25. Ibid., pp. 86-122.
26. Ibid., pp. 186-295.
27. De Kerckhove's personal communication with McLuhan.
28. Marchand, (1998), op. cit., p. 151
29. Ibid., p. 184
30. Gerald Emanuel Stearn, *McLuhan Hot & Cool* (New York: The Dial Press, Inc., 1967), p. 45.
31. Barrington Nevitt and Maurice McLuhan, eds. (1995), op. cit., pp. 29-30.

Chapter 2: What Haven't You Noticed Lately?

1. McLuhan (1964), op. cit., p. 26.
2. Ibid.
3. See, for example, "Jeffrey Wigand, Ph.D. The Insider" at http://www.jeffreywigand.com/ and "States and Tobacco Industry Reach Landmark Settlement" at http://www.courttv.com/legaldocs/business/tobacco/settlement.html.
4. Marshall McLuhan, *Understanding Media: The Extensions of Man*, with an Introduction by Lewis Lapham (Cambridge: MIT Press, 1994), p. xi.
5. McLuhan (1964), op. cit., p. 8.
6. See, for example, "Apple's New Message: Clone This!" at http://www.zdnet.com/zdnn/content/zdnn/0903/zdnn0002.html, or "Apple's Clone Support in Question" at

http://www.macworld.com/
1997/06/news/3740.html.

7. Salesman's folk saying, often
heard by author Mark
Federman in sales
conferences.

8. "The Seven O'Clock Show,"
CBC Television, 1967

9. W. Terrence Gordon,
McLuhan for Beginners (New
York: Writers and Readers
Publishing, Inc., 1997),
p. 34.

CHAPTER 3: ALL THE WHIRLED, A STAGE

1. Carroll, Lewis, *More
Annotated Alice: Alice's
Adventures in Wonderland and
Through the Looking Glass and
What Alice Found There, with
Notes by Martin Gardner*
(New York: Random House,
1990), p. 253. Martin
Gardner's annotation on this
phrase is additionally
illustrative. He refers to an
article by Lewis Carroll,
"The Stage and the Spirit of
Reverence," in which Carroll
notes: "No word has a
meaning *inseparably* attached
to it; a word means what the
speaker intends by it, and
what the hearer understands
by it, and that is all. ... [I]t is
a comfort to remember
[language] is often a mere
collection of unmeaning
sounds, so far as speaker and
hearer are concerned."

2. George Orwell, *1984: A
Novel* (London: Secker &
Walburg, 1962), p. 46.

3. McLuhan, (1964), op. cit.,
p. 8.

4. McLuhan maintained that
the speed-up caused by
electric technologies
"retribalized" man, leading
to the metaphor of the
"Global Village." See, for
example, the chapter on
"Radio" in McLuhan (1964),
p. 297 ff., or Marshall
McLuhan and Quentin
Fiore, *War and Peace in the
Global Village; an inventory of
some of the current spastic
situations that could be
eliminated by more
feedforward*. (New York:
McGraw-Hill, 1968) or Eric
Norden, "A Candid

Conversation with the High
Priest of Popcult and
Metaphysician of Media,"
Playboy, (March 1969).

5. Marshall McLuhan,
*Understanding Media: The
Extensions of Man*, with an
Introduction by Lewis
Lapham, (Cambridge: MIT
Press, 1994), p. xi.

6. Marshall McLuhan and
Wilfred Watson, *From Cliché
to Archetype* (New York:
Viking Press, 1970),
pp. 30-34.

7. George Orwell, *Animal Farm*
(London:Seeker & Warburg,
1962), p. 105.

8. Based on the personal
experience of the author
Mark Federman who was a
sales colleague at HDS
during this brief period in
its history.

9. Personal communication
with the author Mark
Federman.

10. McLuhan and Watson
(1970), op. cit., particularly
pp. 12-15, 30-34, 45-46.

11. Ibid., p. 34.

12. Ibid., p. 54

13. Ibid.

14. Based on William
Shakespeare's famous
monologue from Act II,
Scene VII, *As You Like It*.

15. McLuhan and Watson
(1970), p. 15.

16. Ibid., p. 54

17. Ibid., particularly pp. 40-41.

18. Edward T. Hall, *The Silent
Language* (New York:
Doubleday, 1959), p. 248.

19. Don Tapscott and Art
Caston, *Paradigm Shift: The
New Promise of Information
Technology* (New York:
McGraw-Hill, 1993).

20. McLuhan and Watson
(1970), p. 133.

CHAPTER 4: INTRODUCING A NEW CRYSTAL BALL

1. Marshall McLuhan and Eric
McLuhan, *Laws of Media:
The New Science* (Toronto:
The University of Toronto
Press, 1988), p. 239.

2. McLuhan and Nevitt (1972),
p. 16.

3. Ibid., p. 20.

4. Robert Andrews, ed., *The
Columbia Dictionary of
Quotations*, (New York:
Columbia University Press,
1995).

5. Ira Sager, "Big Blue at Your
Service," *Business Week*, July
21, 1999. Available at http://
www.businessweek.com/
archives/1999/b3634014.htm.

6. For an interesting, in-context
perspective on bundling PCs
and servers with a large
services contract see Michael
Kanellos, "Is HP-Compaq
Really a Bad Idea?" at http://
news.cnet.com/news/
0-1272-210-7395750-1.html
(October, 2001). In
particular, Kanellos notes:
"PCs. They are ubiquitous,
disposable, imitative,
anonymous, unprofitable and
ultimately indispensable.
Multimillion-dollar
corporate contracts may
involve process re-
engineering consulting
projects and ingenious e-
commerce applications. But
the deals often hinge on the
ability of an IBM or an HP
to air-drop 35,000 identically
configured desktops,
notebooks and generic
Wintel servers at any given
point on the globe. ... As
one former IBM executive
burbled at a trade show
cocktail party once:
'PCs...They are a
necessary evil.'"

7. Ibid.

8. Sager (1999) op. cit.

9. McLuhan (1964) op. cit.,
p. 251

10. Chris Argyris, "Good
Communication That Blocks
Learning," *Harvard Business
Review*, Volume 72, Number
4, July-August, 1994,
pp. 77-85.

11. Ibid., p. 80.

12. Ibid.

13. Ibid., p. 81.

14. McLuhan and Nevitt (1972),
p. 16.

15. Marshall McLuhan, *Culture
Is Our Business*, (Toronto:
McGraw-Hill, 1970), p. 184.

16. Marshall McLuhan,
correspondence to Jonathan

Miller, April 22, 1970.

Molinaro, McLuhan and Toye, *Letters of Marshall McLuhan.* (Toronto: Oxford University Press, 1987), p. 405.

17. McLuhan and McLuhan (1988) op. cit., pp. 98-99.

18. Ibid., p. 129.

19. McLuhan (1964), p. 57.

20. Marshall McLuhan and Quentin Fiore, *The Medium is the Massage,* (New York: Random House, 1967), p. 40.

21. McLuhan and McLuhan (1988), op. cit., p. 100.

22. Donella Meadows, et. al., *The Limits to Growth: A report for the Club of Rome's project on the predicament of mankind* (New York: Universe Books, 1974).

23. Derrick de Kerckhove, *Brainframes* (Utrecht: Bosch & Keuning, 1991), p. 89.

24. Herman Kahn's computer model.

25. Marshall McLuhan (1964), p. 60.

26. McLuhan and McLuhan (1988), p. 99.

CHAPTER 5:
THROUGH A GLASS DARKLY

1. McLuhan and McLuhan (1988), p. 228.

2. Personal conversation with Eric McLuhan.

3. See McLuhan and McLuhan (1988), p. 98. In particular, they note that, "Our Laws of Media do not rest on any concept or theory, but are empirical ... All four aspects are inherent in each artifact from the start."

4. McLuhan and Fiore (1967) op. cit., p. 25.

5. Marketing and sales executives in Apple at the time emphasized the handwriting recognition feature above any other capability, despite engineering advice to the contrary, indicating their subconscious view of the Newton as an extension of the notepad. For two engineering insiders' views

see Andrew Gore, "Feet of Clay: The Newton's death should be a lesson for Apple," *MacWorld – The Vision Thing* at http://www.macworld.com/1998/05/opinion/4293.html, or Larry Tesler, "Why the Apple Newton Failed," *TechTV – The Screen Savers*, at http://www.techtv.com/screensavers/showtell/story/0,24330,3013675,00.html.

6. McLuhan (1964), p. 8.

7. Gordon (1997) op. cit., p. 34.

8. McLuhan and Fiore (1967), p. 125

CHAPTER 6:
"WE SHAPE OUR TOOLS AND THEREAFTER OUR TOOLS SHAPE US"

1. Larry Kanter, "Marketing Decisions are the Most Important," *Business Week Online*, at http://www.businessweek.com/smallbusiness/content/jun2001/sb20010618_984.htm.

2. Ibid.

3. Ed Garsten, "Slow selling Aztek gets a boost from "Survivor," *The Detroit News*, at http://www.detnews.com/2001/autos/0104/autos-217892.htm.

4. April 26, 2001 episode.

5. Television Preview is actually the Evansville, Indiana market research firm, "RSC the Quality Measurement Company." See Zach Dubinsky, "Spot the TV Ad", *NOW Magazine*, September 7-13, 2000 issue, available at http://www.nowtoronto.com/issues/2000-09-07/news2.html.

6. Correspondence accompanying the $40 cheque to a raffle winner.

7. McLuhan (1964), p. 18.

8. Anthony B. Perkins, "The Angler: Mending the Net", *Red Herring*, September 15, 2001, available at http://www.redherring.com/mag/issue104/167645.html.

8. McLuhan and McLuhan (1988), op. cit., p. 228.

9. Ibid, p. 98.

10. Marshall McLuhan (1964), p. 346.

11. Ibid., p. 26.

12. See McLuhan and McLuhan, op. cit., pp. 130, and for examples, see p. 208-214. Especially enlightening are the examples of Aristotelian through Newtonian Laws of Motion and Einsteinian Space-Time Relativity.

CHAPTER 7:
BUSINESS HOT AND COOL

1. McLuhan (1964), p. 44, ff.

2. Corey Grice, "CEO Hancock Out at Exodus," *CNet News.com*. http://www.news.com/news/0-1004-200-7053395.html.

3. Ben Elgin, "Making Her Own Luck," *Business Week e.biz*, November 20, 2000. Available at www.bw.com/2000/00_47/b3708040.htm.

4. Ibid.

5. Exodus Executive Forum, Toronto, April 14, 2001.

6. Garten, Jeffrey. "Jack Welch: A Role Model for Today's CEO?," Business Week. September 10, 2001. Available at http://www.businessweek.com/magazine/content/01_37/b3748029.htm. Visited December, 2001.

7. Brady, Diane. "This is Just About the Best Gig You Can Have," Business Week Daily Online. September 5, 2001. http://www.businessweek.com/bwdaily/dnflash/sep2001/nf2001095_136.htm. Visited September, 2001.

8. Ira Sager, "Big Blue at Your Service," *Business Week*, July 21, 1999. Available at http://www.businessweek.com/archives/1999/b3634014.htm.

9. See, for instance, Peter Burrows, "The Radical: Carly Fiorina's Bold Management Experiment at HP," *Business Week*, February 19, 2001, available at http://www.businessweek.com/2001/01_08/b3720001.htm;

and Peter Burrows, "Commentary: HP's Woes Are Deeper than the Downturn," *Business Week*, May 7, 2001, available at http://www.businessweek.com/magazine/content/01_19/b3731061.htm.

10. Anthony Bianco and Pamela L. Moore, "Xerox: The Downfall — The Inside Story of the Management Fiasco at Xerox," *Business Week*, March 5, 2001.

11. Marshall McLuhan, correspondence to Jonathan Miller, April 22, 1970. Molinaro, McLuhan and Toye, *Letters of Marshall McLuhan* (Toronto: Oxford University Press, 1987), p. 405.

12. Kerry Capell, Catherine Arnst and Arlene Weintraub, "At Risk: A Golden Opportunity in Biotech," *Business Week*, September 10, 2001. Available at http://www.businessweek.com/magazine/content/01_37/b3748095.htm.

Chapter 8: "Humpty Dumpty Together Again"

1. McLuhan (1964), p. 183.
2. Ibid.
3. Ibid., p. 352.
4. Ibid., p. 350.
5. Ibid., p. 348.
6. McLuhan and Nevitt (1972), p. 256.
7. Ibid.
8. Gareth Morgan, *Images of Organization* (Beverly Hills: Sage Publications, 1986.), p. 78.
9. Ibid. p. 79.
10. Ibid. p. 102.
11. Adapted from Gareth Morgan (1986), p. 103.
12. Marshall McLuhan (1964), p. 351.
13. McLuhan and Nevitt (1972), p. 76.

The End of the Beginning

1. Robert Andrews, ed., *The Columbia Dictionary of Quotations* (New York: Columbia University Press, 1995).
2. McLuhan (1964), p. 277.
3. McLuhan and Fiore (1967), p. 25.

Bibliography

—. *The Complete Works of William Shakespeare*. New York: Avenel Books, 1975.

Andrews, Robert, ed. *The Columbia Dictionary of Quotations*. New York: Columbia University Press, 1995.

Argyris, Chris. "Good Communication That Blocks Learning," *Harvard Business Review*. Volume 72, Number 4, July-August, 1994.

Bianco, Anthony and Moore, Pamela L. "Xerox: The Downfall — The Inside Story of the Management Fiasco at Xerox," *Business Week*, March 5, 2001.

Brady, Diane. "This is Just About the Best Gig You Can Have," *Business Week Daily Online*. September 5, 2001. http://www.businessweek.com/bwdaily/dnflash/sep2001/nf2001095_136.htm. Visited September, 2001.

Burrows, Peter. "The Radical: Carly Fiorina's Bold Management Experiment at HP," *Business Week*, February 19, 2001. http://www.businessweek.com/2001/01_08/b3720001.htm. Visited December, 2001.

Burrows, Peter. "Commentary: HP's Woes Are Deeper than the Downturn," *Business Week*. May 7, 2001. http://www.businessweek.com/magazine/content/01_19/b3731061.htm. Visited December, 2001.

Capell, Kerry and Arnst, Catherine and Weintraub, Arlene. "At Risk: A Golden Opportunity in Biotech," *Business Week*. September 10, 2001. http://www.businessweek.com/magazine/content/01_37/b3748095.htm. Visited December, 2001.

Carroll, Lewis. *More Annotated Alice: Alice's Adventures in Wonderland, and Through the Looking Glass and What Alice Found There*, with Notes by Martin Gardner. New York: Random House, 1990.

Dubinsky, Zach. "Spot the TV Ad," *NOW Magazine*. September 7-13, 2000. http://www.nowtoronto.com/issues/2000-09-07/news2.html. Visited November, 2001.

Elgin, Ben. "Making Her Own Luck," *Business Week e.biz*. November 20, 2000. Available at http://www.bw.com/2000/00_47/b3708040.htm. Visited September, 2001.

Garsten, Ed. "Slow selling Aztek gets a boost from "Survivor"," *The Detroit News*. http://www.detnews.com/2001/autos/0104/autos-217892.htm. Visited December, 2001.

Garten, Jeffrey. "Jack Welch: A Role Model for Today's CEO?," *Business Week*. September 10, 2001. Available at http://www.businessweek.com/magazine/content/01_37/b3748029.htm. Visited December, 2001.

Gordon, W. Terrance. *Marshall McLuhan: Escape into Understanding, A Biography*. New York: BasicBooks, A Division of HarperCollins Publishers, 1997.

Gordon, W. Terrence. *McLuhan for Beginners*. New York: Writers and Readers Publishing, Inc., 1997.

Gore, Andrew. "Feet of Clay: The Newton's death should be a lesson for Apple," *MacWorld – The Vision Thing*. http://www.macworld.com/1998/05/opinion/4293.html. Visited September, 2001.

Grice, Corey. "CEO Hancock Out at Exodus," CNet News.com. http://www.news.com/news/0-1004-200-7053395.html. Visited September, 2001.

Hall, Edward T. *The Silent Language*. New York: Doubleday, 1959.

Hammer, Michael and Champy, James. *Reengineering the Corporation: A Manifesto for Business Revolution*. New York: HarperBusiness, 1993.

Kanellos, Michael. "Is HP-Compaq Really a Bad Idea?," CNet News.com Perspectives. http://news.cnet.com/news/0-1272-210-7395750-1.html. Visited October, 2001.

Kanter, Larry. "Marketing Decisions are the Most Important," Business Week Online. http://www.businessweek.com/smallbusiness/content/jun2001/sb20010618_984.htm. Visited December, 2001.

Marchand, Philip. *Marshall McLuhan, The Medium and the Messenger*. Cambridge, MA: The MIT Press, 1998.

McLuhan, Marshall. *Culture Is Our Business*. Toronto: McGraw-Hill Book Co., 1970.

McLuhan, Marshall. *The Mechanical Bride: Folklore of Industrial Man*. Boston: Beacon Press, 1967.

McLuhan, Marshall. *Understanding Media: The Extensions of Man*. New York: McGraw-Hill, 1964.

McLuhan, Marshall. *Understanding Media: The Extensions of Man*, with an Introduction by Lewis Lapham. Cambridge: The MIT Press, 1994.

McLuhan, Marshall and Fiore, Quentin. *The Medium is the Massage*. New York: Random House, 1967.

McLuhan, Marshall and Fiore, Quentin. *War and Peace in the Global Village: an inventory of some of the current spastic situations that could be eliminated by more feedforward*. New York: McGraw-Hill, 1968.

McLuhan, Marshall and McLuhan Eric. *Laws of Media: The New Science*. Toronto: The University of Toronto Press, 1988.

McLuhan, Marshall and Nevitt, Barrington. *Take Today: The Executive as Dropout*. New York: Harcourt Brace and Jovanovich, Inc., 1972.

McLuhan, Marshall and Watson, Wilfred. *From Cliché to Archetype*. New York: Viking Press, 1970.

Meadows, Donella, et. al. *The Limits to Growth: A report for the Club of Rome's project on the predicament of mankind*. New York: Universe Books, 1974.

Molinaro, Matie and McLuhan, Corinne and Toye, William. *Letters of Marshall McLuhan*. Toronto: Oxford University Press, 1987.

Morgan, Gareth. *Images of Organization*. Beverly Hills: Sage Publications, 1986.

Nevitt, Barrington, and McLuhan, Maurice, eds. *Who Was Marshall McLuhan?* Toronto: Stoddart, 1995.

Norden, Eric. "A Candid Conversation with the High Priest of Popcult and Metaphysician of Media." *Playboy*, March 1969.

Orwell, George. *Animal Farm*. London: Secker & Warburg, 1962.

Orwell, George. *Nineteen Eighty-four: A Novel*. Toronto: Penguin Books, 1983.

Perkins, Anthony B. "The Angler: Mending the Net," *Red Herring*. September 15, 2001. http://www.redherring.com/mag/

issue104/167645.html. Visited September 2001.

Pollack, Richard "Understanding McLuhan," *Newsweek*. February 28, 1966.

Sanderson, George, ed. *The Antigonish Review* Number 74-75, Marshall McLuhan. Antigonish, NS: St. Francis Xavier University, 1988.

Sanderson, George and MacDonald, Frank, eds. *Marshall McLuhan: The Man and his Message*. Golden, CO: Fulcrum, 1989.

Sager, Ira. "Big Blue at Your Service," *Business Week*, July 21, 1999. http://www.businessweek.com/archives/ 1999/b3634014.htm. Visited December, 2001.

Stearn, Gerald Emanuel. *McLuhan Hot & Cool*. New York: The Dial Press, Inc., 1967.

Tapscott, Don and Caston, Art. *Paradigm Shift: The New Promise of Information Technology*. New York: McGraw-Hill, 1993.

Tesler, Larry. "Why the Apple Newton Failed," *TechTV – The Screen Savers*. http://www.techtv.com/screensavers/ showtell/story/0,24330,3013675,00.html. Visited September, 2001.

Theall, Donald. *The Virtual McLuhan*. Montréal & Kingston: McGill-Queen's University Press, 2001.

Willmott, Glenn. *McLuhan or Modernism in Reverse*. Toronto: University of Toronto Press, 1996.

Wolfe, Tom. *The Pump House Gang*. New York: Farrar, Straus & Giroux, 1968.

Index